GHOST *in* THIS HOUSE
essays from a privileged life

jbuck ford

JBuck Ford

JBuck Ford

For Murph, Jesse, Tucker & James

You think when you wake up in the mornin that yesterday
don't count. But yesterday is all that does count.
What else is there? Your life is the sum of the
yesterdays it's made of. Nothin else.
Cormac McCarthy

I'm just a ghost in this house
I'm just a shadow upon these walls
Hugh Prestwood

JBuck Ford

TABLE *of* CONTENTS

Prologue
On a Writer's Life

Prologue
On a Writer's Life

IN THE SPRING OF 2008, I WAS BLESSED to join the ranks of legitimate authors with the publication of my first book, a memoir chronicling the mercurial and storied half-century marriage of my mother and father, and our family's life in and out of the spotlight. I was fortunate beyond reckoning for a new writer; *River of No Return* was released on the Cumberland imprint to respectable, if not stellar sales, and garnered notices that were both humbling, and, for a writer praying for some kind of sign, persuasive. Publishers Weekly's starred review called it a *"masterfully rendered, compulsively readable"* book, and Library Journal said it was *"compelling and well written."*

I didn't know from compelling—I was too busy exhaling. And praying to God I had at least one more book in me.

Like many freshman writers, I believed that God had imbued me with a great talent; that it was my destiny to place something perfect on a blank page; something that would stand the test of time for generations to come. Through wars and depressions, great scientific discoveries and changes in the balance of world power; through births, lifetimes and deaths I would write perfect words that would live on. Years, decades from now, some seeker of knowledge, a reader, a student, perhaps, or maybe a bricklayer, would come upon the cover of my book, or glance at the spine perchance, and be drawn to it as if it were a magnet. Like an archaeologist stumbling upon what they know instinctively to be a great treasure, the find they've sought all their lives, they would slide the book out of its place between other lesser tomes, regard it with the barely concealed exuberance of a museum curator, open it carefully, and breathe in the gentle exhalation of time and wisdom, fear and love, hope and despair from within its pages, and they would know; they would know deep within the recesses of their hearts, their souls: *I have to read this book.*

Eventually, helped with the right medications, those and other literary delusions all but passed, their story arcs ending in denouements that simply faded away into the light of reality. And the reality was any dream I had of a career as a writer was a non-starter unless and until I came to grips with the fact that being a working writer was just that: work. The problem was it just wasn't the kind of work I was raised to do; the kind of work I could relate to.

It's well documented that many, if not most, writers agree that the human process, the physical act of writing; of sitting down at a table or a desk and pulling up, opening, or placing a clean sheet of paper in front of you, and then attempting to fill its emptiness with words that make sense, is something akin to self-torture. History is replete with the warnings from great authors doing their best to dissuade any and all who were foolish enough, who were sufficiently deluded to believe that they might seek a career in the field. Hemingway was unequivocal: "There's nothing to writing," he said. "All you do is sit down at a typewriter and bleed." When Dorothy Parker was asked by Vanity Fair to comment on her work, she deadpanned, "I hate writing. I love having written."

I can relate.

I am, and have always been happiest when I'm doing manual labor. You haul the wood. You stack it. You dig the hole, you fill it in. Work that's real. Work that I see the results from immediately. Work that draws the sweat out of me. I don't break a single bead when I'm at this keyboard. I don't feel the pain of the work in my muscles, in my hands. I don't need a water break. If I've made any money, it felt like I was, I don't know... cheating. Not doing work I was raised to understand. The kind of work that made me feel proud. The kind of work that made me feel like I was contributing to the greater good of something. Poring over a semi-blank white page and mining the vocabulary veins for words to fill the emptiness just wasn't work. It was creative angst, but not *work*-work.

Then I found a quote from John Dunne that changed all that.

John Gregory Dunne was a man whose life paralleled much of my own. Tough upbringing in a privileged house. Estranged from his brother. Married to a woman equally as talented who saved his life, lost a child in the prime of life and struggled with depression for years, pouring words on the page in a lifelong effort to write himself out of it. His storied marriage to author Joan Didion came close to ending more than once; a relationship pocked with decades of turbulence, legendary arguments, and brilliant collaborations.

Google "Quotations from John Gregory Dunne" and you're likely to find only a handful. It was his take on writing that prompted me to view this work in a different light, and to make it work for me.

"Writing", he said, "is a manual labor of the mind: a job, like laying pipe."

True enough. Save for one tiny little detail. Nearly all the plumbers and laborers I've known—and I have known and worked alongside many—are in better physical shape than virtually every writer I've had the pleasure of knowing or working with. In fact, while I hold Mr. Dunne and his memory in very high regard, I think I can say without fear of any real reprisal, that Mr. Dunne likely had about as much knowledge of the laborious life of a pipefitter l as I do of...oh, the serving staff of the Emir of Dubai.

As writers, we tend to keep ourselves in better shape mentally than physically. We set daily goals, usually measured in pages, paragraphs or word count, and exercise a strict professional and creative discipline to meet those goals. We exercise our imaginations, our eyes, and our fingers in the process, but sadly many of us exercise little else. As time goes on, we tend to take root during our average work day; our posteriors spreading across the seat of the office chair like modeling clay; eventually hardening, threatening to wedge us between the armrests.

Nevertheless, Dunne's blue-collar view of the decidedly white-collar work he did for a living radically changed my own perception. It underscored his Vanity Fair comment that "What a writer brings to any story is an attitude...an attitude usually defined by the wound stripes of life." I suppose one could add that having some basic understanding of the language, syntax, and vocabulary helps, but it's the attitude... the voice you bring to the words you write that really matters. That, and the ability, the discipline, to actually sit down—every day—and physically write. Pen to paper. Finger to keystroke. Something. Anything. I don't write because I want to. I write because I *have* to; I have no choice in the matter. It is tortuous, bitter work, this; obscuring the purity of a blank page; clean and virgin, like new snow, with words blackened in ink. Strung together, for God's sake.

. . . .

I rather like the word *prolific*. I'd like to *be* prolific as much or more than I like the word itself. I suppose drafting a few hundred words of social content for clients four days a week might qualify, but, I don't know. I'd like to read the word prolific next to my name in a New York Times book review. I'd settle for a Pocatello book review.

I'm amazed by writers who can churn out books to the tune of one or two a year. It takes me that long to come up with a title I think works. I suppose that makes me a bit on the obsessive-compulsive side, but I don't care. I care about a title that works. If the title doesn't grip me by the throat and threaten to choke the life out of me, I pass and pick up the one that does. I like visceral titles; titles that speak with authority, that command you psychically to…*Read This Book. Now. Your life…. And a few good hours on the couch depend on it.*

James Rollins writes a book every month. Seems that way, anyway. I reread Stephen King and Cormac McCarthy books obsessively. Justin Cronin's prose is hypnotic. I have waking dreams of constructing sentences as nuanced as Joan Didion's.

And then there's Dean Koontz. The thing about Koontz is a lot of his heroes are writers, or would be writers. Had *been* writers. Has-been writers. Writers in a slump. Writers who've hit the wall. Long, drifting passages describing laptops that haven't been on in a while. Pens that haven't been put to paper, fingertips that haven't depressed keystrokes. Monitors that glow mockingly, empty and void of any lines of text. Books started and left undone, interrupted by some life-changing event that shattered the protagonist forever.

I understand these people. I know these characters he creates. I bought into the whole idea of creating a blog when the trend was the thing to do, but in my case, it had nothing to do with blogging, per se. It was the cue I needed; the prompt to start writing with something akin to daily discipline again. To start writing something... anything, for God's sake. And more to the point, finishing it. I have become literally nauseated by the sheer volume of books, short stories, novels, screenplays proposals, query letters, drafts and half-assed ideas I've started over the past five to ten years and never finished. None of them. They lay in manila files like cold cases in a long abandoned precinct office somewhere. Dead characters and lost goals. Plots that have thinned over time to transparency.

It's embarrassing. People ask what I do for a living... I shrug a bit, and tell them, "I'm a content creator... and umm....I'm a writer".

And I tell them with a straight face, for God's sake.

The essays in this collection were written between 2008 and 2022; each story a stripe from that life; some defined by wounds, others, not so much. Some were pitched to a handful of literary and mainstream magazines, buoyed by the hope of periodical fame. Others not. Most simply languished in the digital depths of one hard drive or another, shuffled from folder to folder like so many literary refugees—each burdened with a past and a tale to tell, and a dream of finding a home between two covers.

I should probably rewrite that last sentence. Sounds a little pretentious.

JBuck Ford.

1.5.25

JBuck Ford

GHOST *in* THIS HOUSE
essays from a privileged life

The Song, the Crossroads,
and the Company Store

Spring 2020

I suspect that most of you reading this will have some knowledge or memory about the song this story is about. You may know one or two lines of the chorus or maybe even a verse or two. You might know some of the story behind it and its composer, Merle Travis, or the impact that it had on the lives of so many millions of people. You might've read somewhere that it was certified as one of the biggest selling single records of all time, and called one of the most important songs ever recorded. A two-minute and thirty-four second chapter of American history, reminding us of the enduring strength of common people and the power of those who would keep them down.

The song was called, 'Sixteen Tons'.

I suspect that some of what follows is part of the story you might not know.

The Song, the Crossroads, *and the* Company Store

BY THE TIME THE SUMMER OF 1955 WAS IN FULL SWING, *Rock Around The Clock* had become the first rock and roll single to reach number one on the U.S. charts. In April, Jonas Salk's polio vaccine was approved by the FDA and Ray Kroc's first McDonald's opened in Des Plaines, Illinois. In May, Chuck Berry cut *Maybelline* for Chess Records and in June, Pete Seeger was subpoenaed to appear for the August hearings of the House Un-American Activities Committee. In July, Disneyland opened its gates in Anaheim, and my old man closed his biggest gig at The Thunderbird in Vegas since he first took the stage there in the winter of forty-nine; a split bill with Kay Starr that sold out every show for an entire week. He and his team would board the Union Pacific Streamliner back to L.A. the next morning, get the last few of the NBC morning shows for the season in the can, then back on the Super Chief for a four week sold-out tour of the Midwest.

By all accounts (if his press agent, Mickey Freeman, had anything to with it) he was killing it. Variety was calling him *'The hottest up-and-comer in show business'.* His last two singles for Capitol broke the

Top 10 Pop *and* Country. His turns as Cousin Ernie on *I Love Lucy* exposed him to a massive prime time TV audience of millions of people, and his own morning variety show on NBC was a hit with every homebody from Sacramento to Schenectady.

But at some point since that first gig in Vegas in '49 (though he was never able to get a fix on exactly when), he'd stopped being an up-and-comer, and had become a property. He was the toast of the town; he was on a fast track up Hollywood Boulevard with the top down. But for Ernest Jennings Ford, youngest son of Clarence and Maude Ford, late of Bristol, Tennessee, the ride had been dizzying, too fast; he'd been white-knuckling the hand-grip all the way and the pedal wasn't even close to the metal yet.

In the summer of 1955, nine out of ten up-and-comers in Holly-wood would've given their eye teeth to have been in Ernie Ford's shoes. But what you want to remember is that Ernie Ford really didn't care. He never looked at himself as an up-and-comer and he never intended to be a star in the first place…it was never his dream. (He told me more times than I can count, "I *fell* into this business, son…"). No, Ernie Ford's dream was that of any ordinary man: regular work, doing the work he loved. But in the short span of seven years, he had become precisely what he never intended to become; he'd gone from an eighty-five dollar a week deejay in Pasadena living the post-war American Dream to one of the biggest new stars in show business. From a man with simple dreams of a normal life to a man whose life was largely no longer his own.

Look, don't get me wrong. He knew a public life meant some loss of privacy; it came with the territory and he understood that. But it had become oppressive to him, an albatross around his neck. He wasn't built to have every moment of every day orchestrated, photographed, scripted and publicized. It wasn't in his DNA. Making matters worse, just as he was beginning to recoil away from the spotlight, he was watching his wife and children gravitate towards it, like moths, morphing into a sitcom family in front of his eyes, reveling in a life that was anything *but* the life he wanted for them. It was the summer of 1955, decades before Leaving Hollywood would become the fashionable thing to do, and Ernie Ford was talking openly of getting out, of seeking a life apart. A life that would take him off this fast-track, take Betty Ford off the cocktail party circuit, and ground his sons in values they would learn in the real world.

Look, don't get me wrong. He loved what he did, but he hated what came with it. Hated the falseness of fame and what he believed living with it was doing to his family. In eighty-four months, he'd achieved and made more than many people would in their entire lives; people he knew worked far harder for far less in work he believed mattered far more. And now, two months before a three hour recording session that would change his life forever, Ernie Ford was questioning the reality of his own success, the fame that had come with it, and the price he was paying for both.

He literally owed his soul to the company store.

. . . .

Ernest Ford was an uncomplicated man, a creature of habit, and he made it a habit for most of his life to stay as far away from politics as he could—if he could help it. He harbored an innate distrust of politicians, politely declined their persistent entreaties, and kept his own counsel. The war was over, he was working, his family had a roof over their heads and the bills were being paid. He came from a long line of Tennessee Democrats, but didn't really have any problems with Eisenhower; had a grudging respect for him, actually, military man and all. Beyond that, he dutifully ignored the issues of the day that didn't concern him; taking pains to avoid both the message and the messengers—religiously. But on a July morning on the soundstage of the El Capitan Theater in Hollywood, in rehearsals for the last week of the season, the message dropped right in his lap.

Historians like to tell us that by the summer of fifty-five, the power of McCarthyism was waning, but they'd be closer to the nut, maybe, to say that the power of Joseph McCarthy, himself, was diminishing. His censure by the senate, coupled with his prime-time humiliation and exposure at the hands of Edward R. Murrow, painted a very different profile than that of the heroic hunter of American Communists he'd portrayed himself as. He'd become a laughing stock in the halls of The Capitol, weakened the legitimacy of the House Un-American Activities Committee, and had been reduced to all but a shadow of his former self.

But the toxic ideology that bore his name did its best work in the shadows, and it was neither waning nor diminishing. On the contrary, it was merely adapting, taking another form, like a mutating virus. Having put the careers of dozens of members of the film, television, and theater worlds on life support, it metastasized, and attached itself to what McCarthy, Hoover, and their allies called *'a wellspring of Marxism in America'*.

Folk music.

Stay with me, here.

Five years or better before the revival that would become the soundtrack for the counter-culture movement of the sixties, the folk singers of the late forties and fifties were writing the protest song template. Woody Guthrie, The Weavers, Pete Seeger, Odetta, The Almanac Singers and others were giving a voice to common folks that had none in the post-war boom that had seen so many of the poor and blue-collared taken advantage of. Working conditions, fair, livable wages and unionization were the themes, and their songs became clarion calls for the rights of the working class. Themes that made their singers unlikely celebrities and the heralds of the burgeoning labor movement; the primary plank in the platform of one of the more popular independent political wings in the country: the American Communist Party. Which put them all in the sights of the FBI, the HUAC, and on the West Coast, in the sights of a growing subculture of hard right Western entertainers and disc jockeys who fancied themselves Hoover's Posse; Singin' Cowboys standing tall in the saddle of the airwaves, defending America against the Red Menace, under the tin star of Christian Fundamentalism, turning their weekly radio shows and live performances into anti-communist tent-meetings, with a few bars of fiddles, guitars and yodeling thrown in to keep the folks in the bunkhouse happy, and to counter the growing din of voices coming from that 'well-spring of Marxism'.

Unknown to Ernest Ford, counted among those voices was a young singer and guitar player who, like himself, had also been discovered by Cliffie Stone, the man standing across from him on the NBC set that July morning in the El Capitan Theater. An artist who'd become one of Dad's closest friends; whose talent had taken the growing Western scene by storm, and made him one of the most popular guitar players, singers and songwriters in Hollywood. A fellow Capitol Records act, he'd been scheduled as the last guest on the last show of the season, and was up for rehearsal, but was nowhere to be found.

His name was Merle Travis.

He'd cancelled, according to Stone. But not for the reasons Dad presumed, regardless of how well he knew, or thought he knew

Travis. And in truth, he knew him pretty damned well. They'd both been regulars on Stone's groundbreaking variety show, *Hometown Jamboree*, both were managed and published by Stone and both were signed to Capitol by Lee Gillette. They'd played hundreds of dates together back in the day, and Travis (along with Jimmy Bryant), had been the go-to guitar player on virtually all of Dad's earliest singles. Add to that the friendship between Mom, Cliffie's wife, Dorothy, and Travis's wife, Judy Hayden, and the bond between the two was only strengthened. They were like a family. But, like somebody somewhere said at some time or another, *'family is always the last to know'*. And in this instance, on this afternoon in the summer of fifty-five, on the darkened soundstage of the El Capitan, flanked by his publicist, Mickey Freeman, and Stone, Ernest Ford was, apparently, the last to know that his friend, his partner, and his brother, Merle Robert Travis, late out of Rosewood, Kentucky, had canceled because he'd been flagged as a suspected Communist sympathizer.

Merle *Travis*.

Word was he'd come up on Hoover's radar eight years earlier, in the summer of '47, when Capitol released his first album, called simply, *'Folk Songs of the Hills'*. A 78 rpm four-disc package of eight songs performed by Travis accompanying himself on guitar, the album predated boxed sets by more than half a century, and would go on to be regarded as one of the most important and influential recordings in history, preserved by the Library of Congress in the National Recording Registry, and establishing Merle Travis as an icon of American music.

But in the summer of 1947, nobody in the HUAC or the FBI was thinking about icons or the brilliance of Travis's fingerpicking style. They were paying closer attention to the last song on the fourth disc; one of five songs out of the album's eight that were Travis originals: *That's All, Nine Pound Hammer, Dark as a Dungeon, Over By Number Nine,* and the last of the five, the song that brought Travis up in Hoover's sights. A song some people in his trenches thought sounded dangerously close to sedition. A song that grew out of Travis's memories of his brother's years working in the coal mines of Kentucky, years long before the unions and miners' rights. Years of backbreaking, lungscarring work deep in the ground and in the pitch. A song that painted a grim picture of life in the mining camp in 20th Century America; a picture of a life just shy of indentured servitude. A song that earned country and folk stations around the Midwest and south unannounced visits from dour HUAC conscripts politely *discouraging* DJ's from playing the song. That it was union propaganda. That it was Anti-American. Or, as J. Edgar himself was quoted as calling it: 'Blatantly Marxist'.

It was called '*Sixteen Tons*'.

Travis had cancelled, Stone said, because they had to send network codes a list of every guest and a list of every song for every show a week in advance. A list that was also reviewed by HUAC adjuncts that scanned for material the government deemed subversive. One of the songs on the list of three Travis was going to perform was '*Sixteen Tons*'. It was flagged, Stone said, and when the network told him to tell Travis to replace it with another song, he bailed.

Dad knew the song, of course; he'd heard Travis play it countless times, onstage and backstage; in front of the mic on the air, and on the Magnavox in our den. He knew the pattern of Travis's picking, and the breakdown at the end of the chorus. He knew the kind of man Travis was singing about; and knew that ordinary people everywhere knew him. He was them, and they were him; he was the classic everyman; he was anyone—man or woman—who struggled every day working for a living that never seemed to pay enough to *make* a living. Common people—people made out of muscle and blood and skin and bone. That's who and what this song was about; and in Ernie Ford's heart and mind that morning on that darkened soundstage, if that added up to sedition, then so be it.

. . . .

While he rarely, if ever, spoke about this moment—this chapter—in his life and career, the full weight and impact of the news and the reason behind it rocked Dad to his core. Like him, Travis was a vet; they'd both served their country—honorably—and wouldn't hesitate to put the uniform on again, if asked. That anyone, particularly anyone in the government, would question what color Merle Travis bled was beyond Ernest Ford's understanding, but not his anger threshold. He was, in a word, furious; furious he'd allowed himself to be so blind to what was happening, furious that such a thing could be happening in his lifetime, and furious that it had landed on his own doorstep.

Against Stone's advice, he put a hold on rehearsals and left the soundstage and Hollywood Boulevard for Travis's little place just outside Woodland Hills, hoping for some kind of resolution, hoping for his partner to reconsider, hoping for maybe a drink, and hoping for the two of them to saddle up, ride into the sunset, and back to the soundstage together.

But Travis was adamant. It was the principal of the thing; these people were calling him a subversive, a communist sympathizer, over a song none of them understood—and no amount of heart-to-heart, money, or bourbon was going to change his mind. Dad urged him not to back down, to stand on his principles. That it was one of the best songs he'd ever written, and folks needed to hear it. But Travis told him he didn't have any choice. *But hell, Ford,* he told Dad as he was leaving, *you like the damned song so much, you sing it.*

. . . .

Back at the theatre, the decision was made to fill Travis's slot with regulars; Molly Bee and Joanne Drew would partner with Dick Farrell for a trio thing they'd been rehearsing, and Dad would cover with one of the numbers off the last EP. The songs filled the hole, the team in the booth was thumbs-up, the cast and crew were good, and Stone was happy. They had a new script, they had a day off, and an early call on Friday for the last show of the season.

And then, Ernie Ford did something that would flip that script and begin a series of events that would change his life forever.

Cornering his bandleader, Jack Fascinato, in his dressing room, Dad placed a copy of Travis's *'Folk Songs of the Hills'* set in Jack's hand, and gave him the nickel version of what he wanted to do. *'I wanted Jack to work his magic; I asked him to take a finger-picking song with a quick tempo for a tenor, slow it down a little, and arrange it for a baritone.'*

None of which was a problem for Jack Fascinato; the man was a musical genius. The problem came up when Dad told him he needed it by the morning, and wanted to rehearse it with the band—at the house—the next day.

And then he told him why. And then, knowing he couldn't keep Stone in the dark, he told *him*.

'I told him he was making a mistake', Stone told me in '91. *'It wasn't about Travis anymore…Ford was putting himself in jeopardy.'*

But Ernie Ford was determined. It was most *definitely* about Travis, he told Stone; his friend was being wronged, and he going to do something about it, the outcome be damned.

But none of them, neither Stone, nor Jack, nor Dad, or Travis could have ever imagined the outcome. Within minutes after the last notes of the song faded away from the soundstage that Friday morning, and from the screens of Philcos and RCA consoles in dens and family rooms across the country, the telephone lines at NBC began melting. Hundreds of calls were coming in by the hour. Within days, a separate office was commandeered to handle the overflow of fan mail. Before he'd left town for a short tour of the Midwest, the Los Angeles HUAC was threatening to force NBC to cancel the morning show and to censure my old man.

But it was too late; the barn door was open and the horse was gone.

．．．．

When he came off the road at the end of August, three things were waiting for him at the office on Gower: a Western Union satchel with some four-hundred telegrams and a shipping container from the NBC mail department with more than 20,000 fan letters; virtually every piece of mail and every wire about the song. That it had touched a nerve was an understatement.

The third item was a *single* letter; this from Capitol's legal department, cordially reminding him that his contract was up for renewal, but he was behind on his recording schedule, and needed to cut two sides by the end of September, or he'd be in breach.

Welcome home from your record label.

Exhausted, he went into a meeting two days later with Stone, Fascinato, and Lee Gillette to pick the sides. Stone arrived with a shoebox full of fan letters and telegrams.

'Ford, Jack and I thought it was a no-brainer,' Stone told me. *'We had a hit and we hadn't even recorded it yet. It was like a shot in the arm—for Travis and Ford. We felt like the label couldn't say no.'*

But that was exactly what Lee Gillette came back with. He'd earmarked an old tune from Bob Merrill and Terry Shand called, *'You Don't Have To Be a Baby To Cry'*, that Ernest Tubb had cut some three years earlier; a country thing that Jack took and completely revamped, changing the tempo, dropping the register, and hipping it up with a horn line and a Big Band feel that just killed it. They'd done it on the morning show a few months earlier, and on a handful of club dates, and the crowds loved it. Gillette was sold on making it the A-side.

Yes, he'd seen the morning show turn on the Travis number, and yes, he dug it and thought Jack did a great arrangement, and yes, he thought it might do well on the charts. But the decision was out of his hands. The Government blowback from the show had reached the label, making the decision for them. It wouldn't matter if there were cratesfull of letters; it was too hot, Gillette told them, too controversial. *'Too communistic'* is how he put it. It'd be the worst kind of mistake the label could make, he said, and it'd be the end of Ernie Ford's recording career.

But the threat backfired, taking Gillette, Fascinato and Stone by surprise, when Dad stood, and put his contract from the label's legal department on Gillette's desk. *It'll be the end of my career with this company if I don't record it*, he said. He looked to Stone. *They can't hold me in breach if I don't renew, right?* He asked him. But Stone, like everyone else in the room was too slack-jawed to answer. Ernest Ford was drawing the line. He'd made Capitol Records more money than they could ever possibly count and he knew it. He was one of their biggest acts, and he was walking, willing to give it all up for a song. For a principle. For a friend.

When he left Gillette's office on Melrose, he didn't expect to return. In fact, he meant not to. He'd done what he could but now he was just…done. Done with the pressure, the stress, the fame, the politics, all of it. He put the top down and turned the radio up, and he could feel the weight of it all sliding off of him. By the time he took the on-ramp to 101, he was making plans to go to the lake with Mom. Maybe even take a look at that little ranch he'd heard was for sale.

But when he walked in the house, Mom was waiting in the kitchen with the phone in her hand.

Gillette and the label had blinked.

It was a compromise, of course; the label agreed to the cut, but it'd go on the B-side, and Gillette knew, hell, everybody knew, that the hard truth of the record business in 1955 was that putting anything on the B-side was a death sentence. Songs were forgotten in weeks, if not earlier, depending on the PR push and the popularity of the A-side.

'None of that mattered to your Dad,' Stone told me late in 1990. *'He stood up for what he believed was the right thing to do. He didn't give a flip about the politics, or the threats, or what was on the A or B side or any of the rest of it. He stood up for the principle, for the song and for Travis. End of story.'*

But it was far from the end of the story.

....

Gillette booked Studio A on Melrose for 10 am on Saturday morning, September 17th. The session was all but effortless; with no time to book rehearsals and hire Capitol's A-team of session players, Jack brought in the band from the morning show. Six cats that knew both numbers backwards and forwards. Everything'd be cut live, no overdubs, no background vocals. Dad, Jack, and a six-piece band. They ran through a few bars of each for levels, and in three short hours they were wrapped, casing axes, lighting smokes and listening to playbacks.

On Monday, the mastered tracks went to press, and on October 1st, Capitol shipped the first promo copies to radio flagship stations nationwide, confident that Ernie Ford had his next hit with *'You Don't Have To Be a Baby To Cry'*. And this is where the lines begin to blur, where the historical narrative becomes intertwined with lore.

No one could ever say for certain, but the prevailing myth still stands today that it was a DJ in Kansas City, manning his morning shift at KMBC when the mail arrived on an already cramped corner of his control board, and...

He grabs the first package on the stack and opens it. Inside is a .45 record. The single. He opens a promo one-sheet inside, his eyes landing on what he needs to know: the A side. He flips the record to 'Baby', just as a commercial ends, and leans into his mic. 'And now the newest record from Capitol recording artist, Tennessee Ernie Ford. It's a swinger called, 'You Don't Have to Be a Baby to Cry'. Hit or miss? The lines are open!' *He kills his mic, but as he does the record slips from his hand. He saves it from falling, but doesn't know he's inadvertently flipped it. He quickly drops it on the turntable, and lowers the needle down. In seconds, the first bars of* 'Sixteen Tons' *fill the room.*

. . . .

Hard-core record collectors, music historians and pop culture curators tend to skip over the fact that the success of *'Sixteen Tons'* was a fluke; an accident. They focus instead on the numbers when the subject of the song arises; that less than two weeks after its release, nearly half a million copies are sold. In twenty-four days, more than a million. By December 15 (less than two months after its release) more than 2,000,000, making it the fastest selling record in Capitol's history, and for years after its release, the most successful single ever recorded.

But the impact couldn't be measured in numbers alone. The song became a cultural phenomenon, finding its way into newscasts, television programs and ad campaigns. Its chorus became part of the national dialogue; a rallying cry for anybody in debt, that owed more than they could ever hope to repay; to the bank, the credit card company, the bail bondsman. Every line spoke to every American, regardless of their station in life. By the end of 1956, it had become the single most influential thread in the fabric of American popular music, etching the names of Ernest Ford and Merle Travis into the annals of history.

But in the heart, mind and soul of Ernie Ford, the impact ran much deeper. It became his signature, attached to him at the cellular level. The song that would accompany his life for the rest of his life. It was, as I look back now, the best and the worst thing that could have possibly happened to him. I look back, and imagine… imagine that the session had never happened. That he'd simply left Gillette's office that day and kept driving. Picked up Mom, Brion and me and kept driving, never looking back, the highway stretching out before him; Hollywood, the business, the fame—all of it—slowly disappearing in his rear-view mirror.

Ghost *in* This House

Fall 2015

Ghost *in* This House

MY FATHER WAS A STUDENT OF MUSIC, an American singer, raised on The Methodist Hymnal, trained in opera, a devotee of western swing and hillbilly boogie—and a cat who knew the difference between the two. He had an unerring, instinctive talent for recognizing genres; a little-known aspect of his musical education that grew into somewhat of a personal penchant as he grew older, and one I grew to respect enormously.

Particularly as it related to Country music.

. . . .

Ernie Ford was not a country singer. He was a singer, period. But he was a singer who understood musically, culturally, instrumentally and lyrically what made a country song *country*. From fifty-eight, fifty-nine, through...seventy, maybe, it was one of the principal reasons he gravitated closer to Ken Nelson and what was coming out of Bakersfield, and kept himself distanced professionally from the Music Row establishment for so many years. His close friendships with its architects notwithstanding, he held a private, but deep disdain for The Nashville Sound and saw it as a wholesale sellout to remake country music in pop's image. Make it relatable, palatable. Upbeat. Make it relevant.

When the label pushed hard in the early sixties to make *him* relevant, to make him palatable, to mold him into the whole Countrypolitan thing, he pushed back, and in April of sixty-four recorded '*Country Hits...Feelin' Blue*', a twelve-song set of lonesome, brokenhearted standards from Don Gibson, Jenny Lou Carson, Ernest Tubb, Hank Williams, Frankie Brown and Carl Perkins, cut over ten hours with two cats: Billy Strange on acoustic guitar and John Mosher on upright bass. No overdubs. No harmonies. Maybe two takes. Every song. It was, hands down, the best album of his entire career. By bringing each song back to its most basic elements, unfiltered, uncluttered by unnecessary bullshit and unapologetically blue, Strange, Mosher and Dad unwittingly created a work that is both a musical masterpiece of simplicity and a profoundly moving exploration of sadness; a human condition that, along with much more, is profoundly missing from what's being pawned off as country music today.

. . . .

I am neither a scholar, a seer, nor a musician, notwithstanding a handful of years masquerading as the latter. I have no dog in this hunt save for my own opinion, and I'm just bright enough to know that it doesn't matter a tinker's damn what my opinion is. Others have said much the same; others with voices more learned, more distinguished...more celebrated than mine. Voices with the power to be heard far above the din, and even they have come under withering fire. My own voice carries no such influence, and it will be read (if at all) by many who will chalk it up to age, negativity, an unwillingness to accept change.... and the bitter ramblings of a late entertainer's aging son who's hoping for some cheap literary controversy.

Take your best shot. Here's the truth....

There was a time, not all that long ago, when country music mattered; when it mattered as a distinct, singular American art form, and a chronicler of life. There was a time when its poets laureate wove hauntingly true, brilliantly real stories that spoke eloquently on the human condition, and a time when its heralds sang in clear, untutored, compelling voices in the crowded and loud wilderness of popular entertainment.

Today, save for a shrinking handful of artists who still hear its voice, it is, at best, a shadow of itself; an unrecognizable mashup of styles that have so thoroughly diluted the genre, that its very essence is being drained away, its true form and sound—its true identity—lost to an entire generation; filtered out by labels-full of indistinguishable voices, after-market fiddles, uninspired Van Halen ripoffs, and, save for rare, endangered exceptions, empty, vapid songs that are like the Country Charts equivalent of overused Facebook memes.

Not that all overused Facebook memes are a bad thing. Even in its most lucid, literary days, 16th Avenue produced more than its share of them. But they were almost always the exception to the rule. *'Achy Breaky Heart'* was a hit for a lot of reasons, principally because it was the balance track; the *I don't want to have to think about anything 'cept tapping my finger on the rim of the steering wheel and riffing on Billy Ray* track in a year of songs that reflected what the greatest country writers and songs had done for decades; held a mirror up to us all. Told us stories that we had all lived through; stories of loss and betrayal. Of sacrifice and redemption. Stories of hope and resolve. Of social injustice and death. Of the unbreakable bond of unconditional love and of hearts broken beyond repair.

These were the songs that held us, that kept us sliding quarters in jukeboxes, made us pull off the road so we could wipe the tears from our eyes. The songs that etched themselves into our hearts and minds and memories. The songs that told the complex truths of who we were in two minute-long stories even the most uncomplicated of us could understand and relate to. They brought us closer together, and showed us our common humanity. They gave us the emotional soundtracks that scored our lives.

If one uses today's charts as a yardstick, more than half of our common humanity's apparently focused on your girlfriend, your truck, a six-pack, her hair, the moon, that ball cap you've got turned the wrong way and a tractor. Not that hair and a girlfriend are bad things. I've just forgotten what it felt like to have either one.

I'm not so far gone that I think it's gone for good. Even now, deep into the night, this glass all but empty, the radio a low hum from across the room, I hear it…I hear echoes of it coming through the speakers, floating across the ether. I hear it curling around Miranda Lambert and snaking through Chris Stapleton. I hear it channeling up through Patti Loveless and hangin over John Anderson…hovering in the air like ribbons of smoke until it fades away, leaving only faint traces in the room. Like a siren song in my ears.

Like a ghost in this house.

JBuck Ford

The Importance *of* Ernest's Cornbread

Fall 2012

The Importance *of* Ernest's Cornbread

IN NOVEMBER OF NINETEEN AND SEVENTY-SEVEN, my second marriage and quite possibly my life were both saved by an eight by twelve-inch pan of cornbread. Not the metal pan itself, mind you, although had the situation been allowed to deteriorate any further, I may have required it defensively, perhaps to deflect a projectile. No, my salvation laid with the recipe for the pone itself, and its architect, its composer—my father. That he was some two-thousand three hundred miles away when he saved me was irrelevant, and actually, he didn't know he was saving me at the time. Truth to tell, *I* wasn't sure that he'd saved me until after the fact.

Bear with me, it's a long story.

. . . .

I moved to Tennessee in 1976 as part of my Five Year Plan on *How to Fail in The Music Business* — which worked beautifully, by the way. *Phase II: Using Your Publisher's Office as a Second Home* was just concluding when I met my wife, Murphy, and the entire itinerary basically went to hell in a handbasket. I still failed—successfully—but a little ahead of schedule, and not quite according to The Plan.

The story really begins about the time Murphy's father reluctantly agreed to allow me into the family, an event which came to pass some four and a half months after our marriage: an earlier event which we notified both sets of parents about *after* it had happened. Not a good idea, in retrospect. I was suspect from day one; a ne'er do well, a rake, a roué. A transplanted libertine from the West Coast who would have to prove his worth, have his mettle tested, and otherwise convince her father *and* mother that they shouldn't simply kill me out of hand for marrying their daughter unannounced. The *kill me* part came closest to happening one afternoon towards the end of November—the very day I speak of in this brief memoir— when Murphy and her mother both suggested that I ride to Sonny's Bait Shop with my father-in-law, Bratten.

Now, I grew up around bait shops, and naturally jumped at the prospect. No better place on earth for a little male bonding with my new father-figure. And because he knew my Dad was a Tennessean, and had actually fished a good deal in that same part of the country, I figured Bratten would be of the same sort of mind-set.

I kindly figured wrong on that one.

Murph and I had just driven in from Nashville, and I was still wearing my mid-70's Twang Town wardrobe: two-inch platforms, blue stovepipes and a wool-knit tam. Like John Lennon's. Way cool. I had on my favorite snap-button shirt, one I'd bought that summer at the Loretta Lynn Western Wear store. Midnight blue with about a thousand tiny little white stars silkscreened on it. With the tam? Please. The whole look said … well, I don't know, it said *something*. Frankly, *I* thought it said I looked fabulous.

Bratten, however, was of a…differing opinion. I knew this from overhearing the colorful way he was telling my mother-in-law, Jo Bill, that perhaps I should've chosen another ensemble. Something, perhaps, that made me look a little less like an idiot.

He said maybe three words to me on the way to Sonny's. When we got there, he suggested I wait for him over by the minnow tank, that he'd just be a minute. Well hell, the minnow tank was a good twenty-five feet from the counter, where he ambled over and spent the next *ten* minutes be-essing with Sonny, who kept cutting one eye over towards me like we're doing a scene from Easy Rider 2. Finally, he cocks his head towards the tank, then back to Bratten and says, "Who you got there with you, B.H?"

Bratten doesn't turn his head; he lowers it, slowly, like an old horse, his eyes closing briefly as he exhales a long plume of smoke from the Camel that's been alongside the toothpick that he keeps wedged between a coupla molars about halfway back in his jaw. The smoke hits the top of the old glass counter-top and spreads across it like dry ice across a concrete floor. His head shakes side-to-side almost imperceptibly. But before he can say anything, Sonny takes a long pull from his Lark, and fairly spits the smoke out in the general direction of the minnow tank. "And where'd you get that hat, son?", he asks me, the words pumping out with the smoke, like exhaust coughing out of a tailpipe. "Carnaby Street?"

Eventually, Bratten introduced me—as we were driving away—and eventually Sonny and I became friends, but frankly, the whole thing kind of hurt my feelings. I'm a sensitive guy, you know, an artistic hyphenate, and trust me, I was sensing it. I was picking it up like a telegraph. For example, riding back in the Fleetwood I could sense that a nightcrawler would have a better chance of bonding with a small-mouth than me with my new father-in-law.

But that all changed in just a few hours.

It got worse. Much worse.

. . . .

I am not a vain person. I have as big an ego as I need, but, vain? I don't think so. At the time of this adventure, however, I was, maybe, just a *tad* vain. About hair, mainly; mine in particular. Principally because I was losing it. By the day. An aerial shot would have revealed expanding crop circles in the follicle fields of my pate, leaving distressed and bare ground where once grew mighty stands of strands, thick and dark. And wavy. Thick, dark and wavy. In the wake of this exodus, what hair I had left was…retracting; curling inwards at the ends in thinning strings, all a-knot and askew, giving me, when not wearing a hat, the appearance of a simpleton.

When bringing this to Murphy's attention, knowing my wife shared my view of the importance of hair; mine in particular, she smartly suggested we go to Rite-Aid and buy a hair straightening kit for men. "Or maybe women," she said. "We'll see which works best."

On the way back from the strip mall, I drove to Murphy's parents' in a state of almost giddy anticipation; a euphoric hunch that in a matter of hours, I would look like the guy on the front of the Pantene Pro-5 Straightening I box in the plastic Rite-Aid bag on the seat between us. That my strength, my… essence would be rejuvenated, re-awakened. Renewed.

And I'd be able to comb it again.

In today's world of hair care, I've learned that straightening takes nothing more than a shampoo, a conditioner, and voila, you're essentially done. In nineteen and seventy-seven, however, the process was a bit more involved, requiring me to commandeer the one bathroom in the house for a rather extended period of time. A couple of hours, if I remember right. For Steps 1 and 2.

Alone and freshly shampooed, I carefully removed the contents of the box and arrayed them in order of use on the built-in shelf behind the vanity. Conditioners, tools, lotions, applicators, a cool comb (a comb!) and a special silver hat with an elastic band that fit over my head like a watch cap made out of Reynolds Wrap. A *perforated* watch cap made out of Reynolds Wrap. Perforated with scores of tiny little holes not much bigger around than a belt notch.

Like a surgeon prepping for the OR, I fit the cap snug around my head, snapped the elastic just above my ears, cracked opened the bathroom door and signaled Murphy, who was waiting patiently in the adjoining bedroom, keen to hasten the experiment and my new vitality. Together now in the bathroom, a towel caped across my shoulders and the cap upon my head, she selected a tool from the kit's contents that looked like a yarn hook for doing macramé. With the dexterity and speed of a weaver, she deftly thrust the hooked end of the thing through each hole in the cap, rotating it slightly, as if twirling pasta around a fork, then pulled long cables of my hair through every port until the whole field of the cap looked like a rice paddy. Brown rice.

Swiftly, she selected a small tube of straightening lotion from the ingredients and with the Special Applicator, varnished all twenty-five hanks of hair flat against the top of the watchcap, where they'd have to stay for the next hour. Finished, I stood, pulled the corners of the towel around my shoulders, pinching them at my throat like a manteau, and turned to face the mirror.

Which was precisely when Bratten opened the bathroom door.

Normally graced with a stoic visage—a John Wayneian profile and jaw framing resolute, piercing eyes—I watched as the entire plain of his face reconfigured in front of me. His mouth slowly slacked open, like it was being lowered mechanically, a half-smoked Camel hanging somehow on the rim of his lower lip. The ubiquitous toothpick hung on the edge of a piece of bridgework. His eyes followed suit, rotating in their sockets like an Audio Animatronic Disney version of Bratten, scanning from the towel to the bathing cap and then to his daughter. He got three strangled words out, "…What in the—", and then Murphy stepped through the doorway, manhandled him around in the direction of the kitchen and pulled the door shut behind her, muffling his last two words: "…goddamned *hell*….?"

The vocabulary choices one makes when cursing can reveal a great deal, if one pays attention. And as Murphy herded her father to the other end of the house, he was revealing plenty. For example, through the bathroom door, I could hear him revealing to Jo Bill back in the kitchen how badly he'd like to see my license plate disappearing out of town, and our marriage license disappearing in an ashtray.

I looked quickly in the mirror, and then looked at the Panasonic AM-FM LED clock radio on the vanity. I had less than fifty-three minutes left. I had to make a decision. I couldn't very well remain locked in the bathroom for another fifty… two minutes, now, and sequestering myself in the back bedroom until I was presentable was out of the question. I was weighing the pros and cons of sneaking out the back door for a hit off the roach I'd saved from the drive up when Murph walked in.

"You can't stay back here for another hour," she said.

I glanced at the clock radio again and offered that it was actually only going to be more like forty-nine minutes, but having inherited a great deal of the stoicism of her father, Murph didn't see the humor I did. Nevertheless, she was right. I *couldn't* stay back here. I was an actor…a musician… I was an *artist*, for God's sake. Image was *everything*. Everything. And I, by God, was doing something about mine. More to the point, I was her husband. Their son-in-law. I had to find some way, some…tactic of connecting with her father. Bonding with him. Bridging the divide. Closing the gap. Taking his .22 shells away.

I suggested that we start packing when there was a knock at the bedroom door.

"Murph?"

Jo Bill… Murph's mom.

"Are y'all ok?"

"We're fine Mom." Eyes cutting to me. "We'll be right out. Do you need anything?"

"Well…"

And then, like a song from an angel came seven words from Jo Bill Cook. Alone, they were merely seven plain and unassuming bits of language; one pronoun, one objective pronoun, two verbs, one preposition and article each, and one noun. Root terms employable in uncountable ways grammatically, and yet, strung together in the order in which they filtered through the bedroom door, they carried with them a power…a saving grace that seemed to fill the room with light. Seven common parts of speech that held the answer to all my hopes and my prayers. Seven words that would build the bridge to reach across this depthless gulf between me and the rocky, adamantine shoals of Bratten Hale Cook.

Seven simple words.

"I need you to make the cornbread."

. . . .

By the time of this story, the marriage that Murphy and I had was just shy of five months old. Not a stretch, by any stretch, but long enough of a spell that I'd already treated her to more than one pan of Ernest Ford's cornbread over that short half a year. And with the occasional hint from the old man on his own recipe, each pan was better, lighter, and more golden that the last. Being a southern girl, she knew from cornbread, and like me, knew that our ship had just come in.

I stood up, snapped the towel off my shoulders and peeled the Reynolds Wrap cap off my head, leaving a crop of twenty-five saplings of hair still cabled together with straightening solution. I looked at the clock radio. Thirty-one minutes. *To hell with it*, I thought. We're talking about cornbread, here.

I turned to Murph who took one look at me and dissolved onto the bed in near-silent hysterics, tears streaming down her face. I grabbed the ceramic-handled, paddle-styled hairbrush with cushioned and synthetic, round-capped bristles from off the chifforobe and thrust it her hand. "For God's sake," I said, "Snap out of it. I've got a bridge to build."

. . . .

I have no real recollection of how many squares out of that pan of cornbread Bratten ate that night. When I watched both he and Bill sopping up the redeye gravy she'd made with it, I knew that, while there would be (and there were) other gulfs, and other canyons, there was one less to cross than before.

Today, our marriage, along with Bratten and Bill, is gone. For thirty-three years I stood in their big kitchen in Smithville, a Cook in all but blood and name. Thirty-three years of births, deaths, fights. Christmases, Easters and Graduations. Vigils, elections and Fiddler's Jamborees. Thirty-three years of hopes and dreams. Of love and of loss. And all of it…. all of it held together with the most unlikely bindery; the recipe for a family's history, passing down through the years and generations.

…A single pan of Ernest Ford's iron-skillet cornbread.

Thank you, Dad.

57

The Query

Summer 2010

The Query

AS A HOPEFUL FIRST-TIME AUTHOR, I LEARNED early on that the creative distress one goes through writing and finishing one's first book pales into virtual insignificance against the anguish, the dejection, and the desperate measures one will endure to finish one's first query letter and land one's first agent. It is the equivalent of literary self-flagellation, on a par with root canals performed with common household tools and DIY tattoo removal. Most writers I spoke with before finally deciding to publish this essay readily told me they'd rather wrap their mouths around an exhaust pipe than repeat the experience. And while I don't share their general sense of foreboding, I can empathize; my first book took two years to write; the one-page query letter nearly three months.

Three months. Three months to write four paragraphs. Four paragraphs on one page that are more important to an agent than the book itself, because if you can't tell that agent why your book will light up the bestseller list in two of those four paragraphs, they're not going to give a tinker's damn about your two-hundred page manuscript. They've got seventy-three more queries to read. Before lunch.

And that, ladies and gentlemen is the name of that tune. Period. End of paragraph.

Every writer has a story about their first time at the rodeo. This is mine.

. . . .

Like most freshmen, I agonized over researching agents. With the first, *first* draft of my manuscript saved, the query and proposal edited and in the chute, I logged on to the top writer's blogs every day, religiously noting their advice. I lived on *AgentQuery.com*. I followed *Predators and Editors* like it was the Wall Street Journal. I catalogued every piece of information I could find anywhere about every agent alive or dead in the known free world. I queried until I drew blood. I sent out partials like they were coupons.

And then, late in 2006 I was signed by one of New York's A-List agents. He was riding a major bestseller-just-turned-movie, and wrote glowingly about the first hundred pages. He told me I was *"the next piece of his plan…"* That my prose was *"heartfelt, raw, and the pacing was fantastic."* I was a gifted writer, he said.

I exhaled.

Three and a half months later, I finished the manuscript. I wrote for guidelines on formatting. He never answered. I wrote again, assuring him I knew how busy he was, but I was excited about getting the final off to him. No answer. I called the office. The office manager told me she'd relay the message. A week went by. Two weeks went by. I wrote to the associate agent that originally requested the partial. I was getting concerned, I said. Three days later, an e-mail. From someone my e-mail'd been referred to. Someone I'd never heard of. They apologized. My kinds of questions however, were normally routed to someone other than my agent, because "…he was just too busy to answer those kinds of questions." He was definitely "interested" in "seeing" the completed manuscript, though, and they preferred hard-copy, Times 12, double-spaced.

I printed, packaged, sent and waited.

And waited.

Two months later, a single-page letter from the agency arrived in the mail. *"We have been unable to find a publisher for your manuscript,"* it said. *"Accordingly, we're no longer representing your book."*

I was a gifted writer. The next piece of this A-List agent's plan.

I wrote back and asked to be released from my contract. I received no response.

Two weeks went by. I e-mailed my disappointment, asked for confirmation that I could query other agents, and for a complete list of houses that declined. An associate wrote back a week later, said I was free to query. I was released. I never received the complete list, and never heard from the agent who signed me again.

I'd poured my life into this book. Literally. I was devastated.

….

I started building a new query list the next week. I was careful not to re-query and incur the wrath of agents that had already declined. My office became a war room. I devised new strategies. I re-wrote the entire query and a third of the manuscript. I polished every sentence, and every paragraph with a verbal chamois. I assembled the new hit-list, I hit SEND, and I hit the post office.

Almost immediately, partial requests began coming in. It was looking good. I settled in for the long haul, but continued to research new agencies. I bookmarked sites, wore them out, deleted them, then changed my mind and bookmarked them again. I kept a database of the return visits to agent's sites I'd queried and those I hadn't. Two weeks into the campaign, I pulled the database up for a review.

Damn. I'd hit Sharlene Martin's *MartinLiteraryManagement dot com* fifty-three times. I clicked the FAVORITES list and hit it for the fifty-fourth time. Cross-referenced my database. I hadn't queried this agent. And what the hell was this '*Considerate Literary Management for the 21st Century*' thing all about? Literary agents aren't considerate…they're sharks, they're hit-people, they're on the rungs somewhere between lawyers and used-car salespeople. A considerate literary agent? Horseshit. They don't exist.

The testimonials were interesting, though, and…damn…she's got the focus here on the authors, not her, not her site, not her success…her *clients'* success. And damn if there wasn't a NYT Bestseller and…wait a damn minute, here. She's sold sixty-some books, and she's only been in the game *three years*?! God almighty…who the hell *is* this woman?

Let's see, she's in LA – cool. She was in network TV and film production – interesting. And these endorsements from her clients…Jesus, they think she's like, well, hell, they *love* her.

I left the office and traipsed back to Murph. She was on her laptop.

"Know you're busy," I said. "Go to *MartinLiteraryManagement dot com*, and browse this site. There's something…I don't know. Let me know what your gut tells you."

And I headed back to my office. About an hour later, the inter-office phone rang. It was Murph.

"I'd query her. She's handled some great stuff. Nothing to lose here."

I spent another half-hour browsing her site, opened up MAIL, wrote what I thought might be the right greeting, attached the query, hit SEND, and left for a late afternoon after-school class teaching Karate.

Three hours later, Murph came to pick me up. Her eyes were dancing.

"That agent you queried today? Sharlene Martin? She called."

"She what?"

"She called the office. There's a message on the machine."

When I got back to the office, I returned her call. We talked for fourteen minutes. Agents don't have fourteen minutes to talk on the phone with an unpublished writer they haven't signed. This was off the radar. And she was so…*considerate.*

"May I send you a partial?" I asked.

"Actually, no," she said. "I want you to send me the entire manuscript."

I tried to conceal my growing fear of soiling myself.

"I'd happy to be. I mean…of will I course. Oh hell. Yes. Are you sure, Ms. Martin?"

"It's Sharlene. And yes, I'm sure."

"Hard copy or Word?" I asked.

"Word," she said. "Let's save a tree."

That was Wednesday, May 2, 2007.

By the next morning, Sharlene had not only contacted my previous agent, but secured a list of the houses that declined. It was significant, but she sensed something wrong…things didn't add up, didn't make sense. More importantly, she didn't quail, didn't flinch, didn't lose so much as one iota of enthusiasm.

At ten am pacific time, she telephoned me. Again.

"This is obviously all happening for a reason," she said. "But I need to ask you an important question. Would you have a problem with Thompson Nellon?"

"Of course not," I said. "Why?"

"Because I just talked with the head of the company, and he wants to see the proposal. Today."

Three and a half hours later, she telephoned me. Again.

"Are you sitting down?" she asked. I told her I was. I lied. I was glued to the ceiling.

"I just sold your book. I'm flying in to Nashville Sunday afternoon, and we're scheduled to meet with the publisher and the department heads first thing Tuesday morning. He only had one question."

"And that was…," I asked, dropping from the ceiling.

"How many zeroes do we want on the check."

At some point, I realized I'd lost the ability to speak intelligibly. Or to speak at all.

"I've e-mailed the publisher the manuscript, and I'm printing my copy off tomorrow, and plan on reading it before I land on Sunday," she said.

. . . .

I sat down at the computer, pulled the manuscript up, and started reading. Then I started sweating. At some point, I recall my brain beginning to bleed. I plodded, I crawled into the house, back to Murphy. "What the hell is wrong?" she asked. "You look awful."

"I don't think it's any good," I said.

"My God, it's fine. It reads fine. Get a grip, for God's sake."

"No. You don't understand. My syntax sucks, my grammar is horrible. And the second half is like, way better than the first half. I'm going to go kill myself. Hold my calls. O.k?"

I sat back down at the computer, my index finger poised above the DELETE tab, when I heard, "You've Got Mail.".

Sharlene. The meeting with the pub was on Monday now. She wanted to have dinner Sunday night. I hit REPLY. 'Great', I lied.

. . . .

Sunday. May 6. Four days since the query.

Murph and I arrive at the Sheraton. In the lobby, Sharlene is in a cream-white pantsuit, smiling. She is beautiful, I think.

"Beautiful," Murph whispers.

We shake, greet, hug. "I finished the manuscript two hours ago," she said.

"What did you think?" Murph chirped.

"Well…why don't we go have a drink and talk about it," she said.

From somewhere in my sternum, I heard the voice of James Earl Jones. *"Luke.* Sorry… Buck… *it's over. She has to have a drink under her belt before she tells you how bad it sucks."*

My legs felt like they were made of pipe cleaners. Any second, now, I was going to drop face down on the floor of the lobby. Somehow, I made it to the table. We ordered a bottle of Merlot, and I brought it to my lips. From the corner of my eye, Murph was scowling and shaking her head. She turned to Sharlene. "So….what did you think?" she asked.

Sharlene unfolded her napkin, draped it across her lap, took a deep breath and looked up.

"Well," she said. "I absolutely loved it." Murphy smiled in my direction.

"See? All that worry for nothing. What do you have to say for yourself?"

"Can I order another bottle of wine?

PART TWO

Dinner was so-so. Murphy and I both had the plank salmon and realized the next morning it was a tad underdone. Sharlene had the prime rib, pronounced it 'fabulous', and we all concluded with a wedge of New York cheesecake topped with strawberries. Decent, but nothing to crow about. I know from cheesecake. I've tasted cheesecake from Orlando to San Francisco, and it was so-so. The berries thing always ruins it for me. Just the cheesecake, please. Try not to fuck it up by slathering some red sauce on top, thank you.

I drained the last of my glass of merlot, and turned to Sharlene. "You said yesterday you wanted this to be a planning dinner. Did I hear that?"

"You did and I do. I'm doing my other pitch at nine, and we're up at 10:30, but I want you there early. Ten to ten fifteen. We'll yak for a minute before we go in… I'll have a reading on the room and the players by then."

"What does your instinct tell you?" I asked.

She and Murph both finished their wine, and like they were pro-grammed, both placed their glasses on the table at precisely the same time, then looked at me at precisely the same time.

Spooky.

"My instincts tell me they want this book. They got the pre-empt because they want this book. Jesus, they only question Declan had for me was…"

"--How many zeroes," I finished for her. "I know. I'm still sort of numb about that, you know?"

I watched Murphy tilt the empty bottle of merlot to the candle-light, and, disappointed, lower it back to the table.

"But I'm…I don't know…curious. Nellon's niche is Christian. Born again stuff. Faith-based. They're like, washed in the blood, you know? What about the e-mail from Josh Mueller? He wants to know if I'll *'profess' my Christian faith*. Damn, Sharlene. Sorry…darn, Sharlene, are we gonna have to like, hold hands in a prayer-circle and sing 'Old Rugged Cross' and testify before we can sign a deal?"

"God, I hope not," Sharlene said. "But I'm wearing my white li-brarian outfit just in case." She took a last bite of cheesecake.

"What do you need me to do in there, tomorrow?" I asked.

"Sell yourself. Sell the book. And make me a promise."

"Anything, girl. Name it."

"Don't tell them I'm a Jew, it'll scotch the whole megilla."

. . . .

I walked through the leaded-glass doors of the Thompson Nellon Publishing offices the next morning at ten am sharp, made for the polished granite wall on the far end of the lobby, and checked myself in the reflection. New jeans, creases just right. Grey-dress Filas—looking good. All-season sport-coat—lint-free. Izod buttoned at the throat—semi-dressy. I polished my glasses, pressed the up button between the elevator doors, and rode solo to the fifth floor.

"Good morning. May I help you?"

The receptionist was smiling beatifically, but not looking at me. Maybe she'd divined that I was standing in front of her…maybe this was just her way of making visitors—in this case, visiting first-time authors—feel welcome. Smile heavenly. Don't look at them.

I returned the greeting, introduced myself, and gave her the stats. I was early for my ten-thirty with Daniel Declan.

"Let me ring his office," she said. "If you'll have a seat, someone will be down in just a minute."

"Thanks." I stood.

Ten minutes later, Sharlene emerged from her first pitch, accompanied by her client, Michael Glasgow, a writer from Nashville who'd scored a major hit with a true-crime chronicle on the Janet March case. Big case, big book deal, courtesy Martin Literary Management. He had another true-crime saga in the wings, and Nellon was interested. We shook hands, mutually wished each other good luck, and Sharlene rode the elevator down with him.

"How'd the meeting go?" I asked quietly when she returned.

"It went great," she said. "Great. How do you feel?"

"That was *my* line," I said. "I know you want me to sell it, but this is your turf, your gig. I'm a newbie, here, a first-time writer. I gotta go with your lead." She smiled. "So…Sharlene. How do *you* feel?"

The smile left her face. "Like kicking some ass. Let's rock."

. . . .

The conference room was a corner, reflected glass on two sides, and a thermostat that was either on the fritz, or Nellon was doing their conservation thing. Either way, it read 83. It was sweltering.

We followed a polite associate who introduced herself as Declan's assistant. I can't tell you what her name was. But I *can* tell you what her domestic situation was, and I can tell your her history of physical abuse at the hands of her father and her first husband, how the same treatment affected the two daughters of the new man in her life, how they went through the same thing with their bio mom, who eventually abandoned them (I think). How God brought *all four* of them together, and got her a job at Thompson Nellon while he was at it. With benefits. Praise Jesus. God is good, isn't he?

We were there for a meeting and we were getting testimony.

"Can He do something about the heat in here?" I asked.

Sharlene shot me a look that would have withered weaker souls.

Our guide was, apparently, unfazed.

"Let me see what *I* can do," she said.

And like a tent-healer, she laid a hand upon the thermostat, handed us some bottled water, told us to have a "blessed meeting", and left us alone. The door clicked closed, and somewhere above the ceiling panels, in the infinite network of ducts, I heard the sound of cool air moving miraculously into the room.

. . . .

Within a few minutes, a stream of people began moving into the room along with the cool air. I should have taken it as a sign. Sharlene and I occupied one side of the conference table, facing a team of seven of Nellon's people, headed by Declan, the VP who'd asked Sharlene for an exclusive four days earlier in Hollywood. Directly across from me, Josh Mueller (another VP) and the author of the e-mail wanting confirmation of my faith. Nellon's senior editor sat opposite Declan, their head of publicity to my right, and a tag-team of two sales guys across from Sharlene. She took the lead after the introductions, and pitched the book like she'd written it herself. She was passionate, driven, eloquent. When she finally paused, I fully expected Declan to pull his checkbook out then and there. Instead, he reached for his water, sipped from the clear plastic bottle and, looking down at his Blackberry, which had just vibrated, started the first round of questions.

"Jeffrey, I know that everybody here got your e-mail about the use of language in the book… and I'd like you to… kind of walk us through some of that. Give us an idea of any *racy* content…"

"Actually," I said, smiling. "There's nothing *racy* at all in the book. No sex, no infidelity. Nothing… carnal."

Smiles all around the table. *Nothing carnal. Praise God.* Exhaling in unison.

"But there is language—language I'm aware might be offensive to some."

Concerned looks. Brows furrowing. I couldn't stop, though. They asked. I needed to tell.

"I had to accurately portray my mother and father both," I said. "And any portrayal of Betty Ford, any quotations from her, would be inaccurate without the inclusion of the language she was wont to use—and used regularly. There's no use of the *F* word anywhere in the book, but there are significant passages using the name of the One we pray to (I swear to God, I *said* that), and virtually all of those instances are direct quotes from Betty Ford. It was as much a part of who she was as the hair on her head."

I paused ever so briefly. "She was a painter, you know. And she painted with language. Great swaths of blue and purple. From the mouth of Betty Ford, profanity was an art."

Across the table from me, Josh Mueller let out a nervous laugh. Like a schoolboy who's heard a slightly off-color joke in the cafeteria line. And like a contagion, it, trailed around the conference table, slowly petering out by the time it got back around to Publicity and

Declan.

"I want that in the blurb," he said, dialing the laughter down.

Suddenly the sales tag-team was animated. They were talking QVC. Publicity wanted to know about stills and press clippings. Marketing was thinking out loud about product synergy; moving Ford Show DVD's with the book. Around the table, the excitement was tangible… palpable…infectious. I was stoked. At some point, I can't say when, I realized the elephant was gone. Disappeared. Back into the hat.

We stood. Declan reminded everyone that Sharlene had given them an exclusive, and he wanted everybody to focus on getting their acts together for an answer by the end of the week. Everyone smiled. I handed out Christmas DVD's. Smiles widened. Hands clasped. Meeting adjourned.

Sharlene walked with me to the elevator, and we rode to the lobby together. "I think we just sold your book," she said. "Declan wants to have a drink with me at the hotel at 5:30. This looks very, very good. Call me around 7:00. We'll yak."

She gave me a quick hug, a light peck on the cheek, and I stepped out of the lobby onto the hot asphalt of the parking lot. In the late morning heat, it was glistening, like a darkening river. Stepping onto its surface, buoyed by the surety of success and the prospect of imminent publication, I had the fleeting sensation I was walking on water.

PART THREE

It's hard to adequately describe, to limn the sense of ecstacy, reward and pride that comes with the knowledge that you've become a published writer, or in my case, *about* to become a published writer. You're suddenly legitimate; you have credentials, credits beyond the blog, the on-line content, and the volumes of television, radio and social media copy you've dashed off over the years. A book, a book you've *written*, re-written, revised, revised again, sliced mercilessly and finally finished, has had an offer. You can now say— truthfully—"…me…? I'm a writer."

The after-effects of the meeting with Thompson Nellon had kept me groggy for most of the day. I was in a kind of euphoric state; hovering somewhere between disbelief, intoxication and elation. I was on a literary contact high. At my desk, I took the mock hardback I'd fashioned some months before, taking the cover off Oleg Cassini's biography, and replacing it with the cover I'd designed of my book, opened the book and inhaled the scent of ink on paper. If I closed my eyes, I could smell the unmistakable scent of a bestseller. I picked up the phone and called our family company's head honchos Jim Loakes and Paul Corbin, walking them through a play-by-play of the meeting from start to finish. I went through it a third time for Murph. We were packing our proverbial bags. Our proverbial ship had come in.

Late in the afternoon, I called Sharlene at the Sheraton. "I'm bringing a DVD of 'The Mikado' for you," I said. "I know you're going to have a drink with Declan and then dinner with Lisa Wysocky, so I'm going to just leave it at the front desk. I'll call to-morrow before you board your flight home."

At my laptop, I opened the manuscript and began reading. Three hours later, I'd reached page 189. I closed the program, hit SHUT DOWN and closed the computer. Murph's words from three days before were ringing like tiny, silver bells in my ears. "It's fine. It reads fine."

I smiled. She's right. It's o.k.….it's fine. It's good.

For the first time in many months, I slept soundly.

. . . .

At around eleven the next morning, I called Sharlene from the car, hoping her morning meeting was done, and I could spend a few minutes with her. She answered on the first ring of her cell.

"When this whole thing got under way, you told me you were giving Nellon an exclusive until today," I said. "I know you heard Declan tell everybody at the table he wanted to be able to give you a final answer by this Friday."

"Right," she answered. "I heard the same thing."

"My question is…are you going to hold to that, or give them some latitude?"

"I think we need to give them the latitude," she said. "I don't think it'll do anybody any good if I hardball them now, because I think this is on a fast-track. I don't want us to be over confident, you know…but you don't bring the heads of sales and publicity and marketing into a first meeting unless you're serious. I think they're going to make us an offer – I'm just not sure what the number's going to be."

"How did drinks with Declan go?" I asked.

"Fabulous," she said. "He's totally sold on the synergy thing, the book being the anchor product, marketing Ford Show DVD's with it, doing QVC…he's excited. Oh, I forgot. I had a thought, and gave him the operettas DVD with *The Mikado* that you'd left for me at the front desk. He was the only one at the table that didn't get a Christmas DVD, you know…so I told him you made a special trip out here to drop this off for him.

"And…?

"He was blown away. He loved it. We scored. It was way cool."

God, I love this woman. "You're too good, Sharlene. That was strong. I'll put a copy for you in the mail right away."

I was still walking on air, still couldn't believe I'd queried her less than a week ago. "This is like a dream," I said.

"I know," she answered. "I want to wake up at the bank. I Gotta go. I'm packing and off. I'll e-mail you on my layover in Dallas if I hear anything."

When I got back to office, I logged onto *MartinLiteraryManagement.*

I wanted to read through the testimonials from her other clients, get
an idea of length, form, etc., and have something in her in-box by
the time she landed in Burbank that evening. I wanted to give
something back. Something besides dinner and one night at the
Sheraton. A testimonial that would be different from anything else
on her site. A testimonial that would let her know I was a writer
now. A published writer–or, soon to be. Something that would let
her know how grateful and proud I was. I opened up Word, and
typed THE QUERY. The first chapter of this essay poured out onto the screen over the next hour.

At 5:02 central, I hit SEND.

At 7:48 my laptop informed me I had mail. The sender was Sharlene. She'd read THE QUERY. I opened the e-mail.

> **Subject: RE: From Jeffrey Ford**
>
> **Date:** 05/08/07 7:48:01 PM Central Daylight Time
>
> **From: Sharlene**
>
> **To: JBF** *Sent from the Internet (Details)*
>
> You may call me when you receive this. Oh my, this is fabulous!

Fifteen minutes later, *she* called the office.

"I just got Chapter One of your new book," she said.

"Well…it isn't really—"

"—It's fabulous. I want you to keep it under wraps."

"It was really just a—"

"—I think when this whole thing is done, when we get the deal, you write the final chapter, and we sell it to MediaBistro, or one of the literary mags. A diary of the whole process, you know – from query to deal."

"Great," I said. "But I really just wanted to—"

"—Tell Murphy I so enjoyed meeting her. She's a doll. I'll keep you posted. Bye." And she was gone. I let the dial tone drone for a few seconds, and then hung up.

A few minutes later, Murphy came back to the office. I was in my chair, holding the receiver in my hand, staring blankly at the keypad.

"Was that Sharlene?" she asked.

"Yeah."

"Did she like the testimonial?"

"I'm not sure about the testimonial," I answered. "But she loves the new book."

. . . .

Wednesday passed. Thursday's sun rose and set. Murphy and I occupied ourselves with normal business. I finished sending e-mail notes to all the other agents I'd queried, including those with, or who'd requested partials, informing them I'd signed with Sharlene. In hours, my inbox was filling with responses.

"Congratulations. Sharlene's great."

"Best of luck. She's a great friend…great agent."

"Damn. I guess I missed the boat. Good luck."

And a score or more of similar good wishes. Each was a testimonial to Sharlene Martin in and of itself. But she didn't just have this effect on her clients... she'd shined the whole damned industry. In *three years*. She wasn't anywhere near her peak, and I'd been lucky enough to get a seat on the bus...damn.

Friday came and went. No word. Murph was nervous. I told her it was fine...normal, par for the course. Not to worry. "There were seven department heads in that meeting," I told her. "I really don't expect Sharlene to hear anything until Monday."

I was scared shitless.

Monday came and went. Nothing. Tuesday, an e-mail from Sharlene.

> I know this must be dreadful for you. The waiting is always the hardest part. I'll let you know the minute I hear *anything*. Try to stay distracted.

Oh, Jesus. She'd italicized *anything*. That meant she wasn't sure. Now *she* was expecting anything. Including...oh *Christ*. Including a negatory.

I tried to stay distracted. Do what your agent tells you. I called Corbin on TEF business.

"Hell, I want to know what's happening with the *book*!" he said.

"This is the norm," I said. "We'll probably hear by the end of the week."

Loakes was fidgeting in Palm Springs. He'd left seven messages on the machine. I couldn't bear to call him.

For two days, I was tempted to e-mail Sharlene. Murph was adamant.

"Do NOT e-mail her. She'll let us know as soon as she hears something. Do the laundry. Bill your karate students. Work on the screenplay. But do NOT e-mail her. She'll think you're stalking…that you're not stable. Promise me."

"I promise."

The next day I finished Chapter Two of The Query, and ran a copy of the operettas DVD for Sharlene.

"Can't I just let her know her DVD's on the way?" I asked Murph.

"What do *you* think?" she countered. It smells—no, it *reeks* of fishing. Let it go. Do NOT e-mail her. *Je*sus."

"O.k., honey." Murphy left the office. I opened AOL and clicked on SEND MAIL.

> Hi, Sharlene,
>
> A quick note to let you know that your DVD copy of 'Gilbert, Sullivan and Ford', with The Mikado and HMS Pinafore went out today. Sorry for the delay…we had some tech issues to resolve.
>
> Best to Anthony…
>
> JBF

Thirty minutes later, my in-box rang. Sharlene

> Thanks, Jeffrey. I'll call Declan today and find out where we are.

That was Wednesday, 4:08 in the afternoon – central daylight.

Thursday afternoon was busier than normal. The public school I was involved with as a martial arts instructor held its annual day-long Field Day, and, as it's been for the past nineteen years, I was there from morning until the end of the school day. At three o'clock, I said goodbye to the kids and the staff, called Murph, and started the short walk home. It was a beautiful day, cloudless, seventy-five, a light breeze from the west. From inside my hip pouch, my cell rang, twice, three times, a fourth, and then fell silent. Whatever it was would keep, I thought. And as soon as the thought passed, Murph did likewise, pulling about, and swinging back to pick me up. I was looking forward to a couple of hour's down-time before heading to the Dojo for the evening's classes. Life was good.

As is my custom, I headed for the office as soon as we got in the house, opened the screen on the HP, hit the power button, went to the kitchen and nuked a cup of joe from the morning's pot while I waited for the laptop to power up. I set the cooking timer for fifty seconds at high. Got the milk out of the fridge, opened the dish-washer, retrieved a clean spoon, and watched the timer count down the last fifteen seconds on the microwave. Three beeps. One semi-fresh cup of joe. I love technology.

On the way back to the office, my cell played the Chopin piece that lets me know a message is in voice mail. I pulled the phone out of my pouch, flipped the lid and checked the read-out. It was from

Sharlene. At my peak of multi-tasking skills, I keyed in my password on the phone as I loaded AOL. The e-mail opened at exactly the same time her voice-mail began on the speaker-phone.

Nellon had passed.

PART FOUR

For a moment, the passage of time slowed to a standstill; the cursor's wink on the monitor froze on, Sharlene's message on my phone dropped in pitch like a record on a turntable being powered off. I was sure that there was some wire crossed somewhere, some logic overlooked -- some reasonable explanation for why breathing was suddenly so difficult.

I pressed CALL and dialed Sharlene's number. Half way through the third ring, it suddenly cut short, and through the near-microscopic earpiece, I could hear the brief, quick intake of muffled breathing on the other end.

"Sharlene….?"

She was crying.

"I can't believe this," she said. "God, I wanted this so bad. I'm so sorry. I would have nev—"

"—Just a minute. Just a damned *minute*, girlfriend. You're crying? You're *crying*?! There's no crying in baseball! Wait…I mean….*publishing*! There's no crying in book publishing! You're

82

Sharlene Martin, for God's sake. You're the toughest literary agent in town. And you're…. *considerate*. Strike that. You're a shark. A fighter. Get a grip."

Silence.

"Sharlene…?

Nose into Kleenex. Then… "Jesus. You're right."

"What the hell happened?"

"They were worried about your mother…and her—"

"—Language? Her profane—"

"—Her death. The… way she died."

"Her… the *what?*"

"It came down in an e-mail from Josh Mueller. He said Nellon was concerned she didn't… what did he say? Wait a second… let me read it to you… here: 'that *she didn't die in a Christian way. We're concerned about the effect it might have on our core market, and frankly---'''* She paused and exhaled like somebody'd cut the valve stem on her spare. "Jesus, I literally can't believe I'm reading this." She said. "… *'we're concerned about the effect it might have on our core market and frankly, on Ernie's fans. She* killed herself. *She broke a Commandment.*"

For a micro-moment, the sheer absurdity of what she'd just told me hung in the air like a bad one-liner from a washed-up comic.

This idiot wasn't just talking about my mother; he was talking about Betty Jean Ford, who began breaking the Commandments when she was barely out of grade school; who broke handfuls of them before lunch every day. Who tutored me at her feet in the paralyzing beauty of profanity and taking the Lord's name in vain… who wrote the *book* on breaking the Commandments, for God's sake.

For an instant, it hung there.

"*And for that transgresshunn, Betty Jean Ford,*" I said in my best Oral Roberts, "*Is going to go straight to Hayull.*"

We both exploded in laughter.

"Betty Ford scotched this deal, Sharlene. Nellon wasn't supposed to happen. Jack Westholm in New York wasn't supposed to happen. *You* were supposed to happen, Sharlene Martin. This book will stand or it will fall with you."

We talked for a few more moments, tightening our belts and sucking air – taking the edge off.

"Thanks for the pep talk," she said. "Give me a couple of days to regroup."

We said goodbye, and I hit END. A fitting gesture; for all my bravado, I was nevertheless convinced that my career as a writer had died before it had taken its first breath.

. . . .

The couple of days Sharlene needed turned into a week, then two. I moved across the hours in slow motion, wading through them with leaden feet and heart. After three weeks, I was certain I'd never write again. Never write anything. I looked at the keyboard like it was some kind of alien device. Putting pen to paper seemed pointless. Obviously, a published writer was not to be my lot in life. It had all been one grand exercise in literary futility.

I was wrapping my lips around the Toyota's tailpipe when my cell phone began playing the Debussy funeral dirge I'd downloaded a few days before. Ringing and vibrating; buzzing like a carpenter bee hung up and humming in my pants pocket. After the fourth ring, the tailpipe was getting a tad warm, and I knew I had a choice to make: burn my lips off, or answer the phone.

It was Sharlene. "We've got a meeting," she said.

My lips, it seemed, were safe.

"Cumberland. It's a small company. Historical fiction and bios, mainly…"

"Boutique?" I asked.

"More like a closet. But they're legit, and they're interested."

"When?"

"Tomorrow morning. You're meeting with Ron Forster—head of the company, and you're going to love this…. Are you sitting down?"

"Yes," I lied. "Tell me."

"He was with Nellon for ten years. And honey, he's looking for a little hard-cover payback."

. . . .

Friday April 4, 2008 – Nine months later

I was running late, and knew I'd be fighting traffic on the way to the airport. Murph was on a 5:30 Jet Blue leg from Kennedy and I needed to be on the off ramp ten minutes ago. If I took Briley to Elm Hill and jogged down to Donelson Pike, I might could come in the back door, shave ten minutes off and still make it to Arriving Passengers before she got out of luggage.

Wasn't going to happen. I threw the van in reverse, got maybe six feet out the drive and two feet shy of rear-ending a UPS truck pulling in behind me. The driver hit the air horn, spooking a bunch of crows in the big oak tree, and climbed out of the jumper seat, carrying a square box maybe 20 by 20. I grabbed the box, signed the digital…signer-thing, set the box in the well between the seats. Foot on the brake, I put one eye on the driver's side mirror, waiting for the truck to back out, and let my other eye drift to the top of the box. Two-maybe three inches above the address label, a dark red logo, rectangular, a black border encasing five words:

CUMBERLAND PUBLISHING HOUSE

NASHVILLE, TENNESSEE.

I laid my windbreaker over the box and hit the gas.

Murph was standing in the waiting area when I pulled under the awning at baggage. I swung curbside, threw it in PARK, threw her bags in the hatch, threw her in the shotgun, ran to the driver's side and climbed in behind the wheel, just in time for three cars and two parking jitneys to pull in front of us. We were going to be there for a few minutes. Providence.

I reached in the cargo hold, pulled a small pocket knife out, opened the blade and handed the bolster-end to Murph.

"And you're handing me a knife in the airport for…."

"I want you to be the one to do this," I said.

"Kill you for being late?"

God, she's funny.

"God you're funny…. I want you to open this."

I whipped the windbreaker off the parcel, flinging it back to the back seat with the abandon of a magician, unveiling the big reveal.

Three cars ahead, one of the parking jitneys swung out into on-coming and, beckoned by the uniformed security, we inched for-ward before coming to a stop again. Murph's eyes never left the box. She brought her free hand to her mouth.

"Oh my God," she whispered. "When did they come?"

"Today," I answered.

"Oh God…. And you didn't… you didn't open it?"

We crept forward another car length.

"I wanted you to do that," I said.

Loaded with riders, the second jitney pulled out and we pulled forward. Another minute, maybe, and we'd be headed home.

"Are you sure?" she asked.

"I love you," I answered.

With her index finger across the length of the blade, like a surgeon, she creased the tape and the tip of the blade sunk between the seams of cardboard.

"Careful...." I whispered.

Slowly, she drew the knife the length of the tape, cut the ends, folded the blade back in its haft, handed me the tool, and opened the box.

I do not believe that I shall ever forget the next moment; should I live beyond all years, it will never fade from my memory. The moment when she lifted the first copy off the top like she was holding a rare thing, an heirloom, and laid the book on her lap, brushing her hand lightly across the dust jacket.

"I can't believe it," she said whispering. "It's real. This is ... this is *your* book...."

She looked up and into my eyes, her own brimming with tears.

"You're an author."

The last car pulled away, and waved on by the uniform, I put the van in gear, and we swung out onto the road leading home.

With the exception of Sharlene Martin and Martin Literary Management, the names of all publishing executives and literary agents used in The Query have been changed.

The Craft, the Draw, *and the* Pinto

Winter 2018

The Craft, the Draw, *and the* Pinto

I'D BEEN WORKING NIGHTS IN AN UPSCALE liquor store in Belle Meade when this story begins, stocking and clerking for a few dollars north of the minimum wage, while spending my days working at cutting a lick as a singer and songwriter on Music Row, making something south of the same pay scale.

I'd come to Nashville in the Fall of seventy-six, bent on stardom in the music business, convinced that my destiny was intertwined with that of my father; that I would succeed him as any son might succeed his father in the family business, take the standard from his hand even as his own days of brilliance waned, and march triumphantly into the spotlight, where I was also convinced the world waited for me.

Nothing so grand ever came close to happening. There was no standard to inherit, no spotlight to claim. No doors magically opened at the intonation of The Name, no showcases at The Bluebird, no record deals. Adding insult to injury, I was losing my hair. There were no prematurely balding guys getting record deals in town (then) and I wasn't a hat act. And the truth is –was—I had a passable style, but nothing memorable. Nothing honest. I tended to cop licks from other singers I thought were cool. I'd do my best Delbert McClinton in the verses, lean to Dobie Gray for the bridge and kind of a Vern Gosdin/Bob Dylan synthesis on the choruses. If I'd saved a nickel for every time a producer in town told me to *'sing like yourself'*, I'd be writing this from the deck of the houseboat.

But the truth is My Self just wasn't all that great of a singer. He wasn't all that great of an act. Gradually, the window of time to seriously contemplate launching a career as a performer out of Nashville began to close. In the end, I could almost hear the rail and sash sliding inexorably down into the sill-casing, sealing shut with an acoustic, wooden note of finality.

B-flat, if I remember right.

. . . .

Moving into songwriting seemed like a natural progression, a logical career shift. I'd been writing short voice over scripts and ad copy off and on semi-professionally for a few years, and felt I could translate whatever skill I had in drafting pithy thirty-second pieces to pithy popular songs. I had the greatest admiration and respect for Nashville's writers, and hoped that I could use some of the thimble-full of studio cred I'd chalked up as a session singer to leverage myself into a weekly draw at one of the scores of publishing houses up and down 16th and 17th Avenues. It never happened, but in the years that I haunted those doors looking for a deal, I hung out, traded lines, and wrote with the cats that were the very best of that rarified breed of composer, and came away with a street degree of sorts in Basic Composition.

In the mid-seventies, the community of songwriters on the Row was more akin to a colony of expatriate literati; fiction authors masquerading as Top Forty tunesmiths. Mickey Newbury, Bob McDill, Marshall Chapman, Tom T. Hall, Kris Kristofferson – they were literally changing the fabric of popular songwriting in Nashville. Make no mistake, any of those cats could punch out twelve-bar cheatin' songs all day long, but they were more apt to write with John Steinbeck or Tennessee Williams as their inspiration than Hank Williams or Hoagy Carmichael; crafting riveting two and a half minute Great American Novels set to a five-chord rhythm chart; powerful, concise essays on the human condition, told in simply-layered, uncomplicated narratives that immediately conveyed the essence of the story being told. They were creating nothing less than a new genre of literature: novellas you could listen to on a jukebox.

Nothing like it was happening anywhere on the Great American Cultural Landscape, and I desperately wanted to be a part of it. After more than three years in the co-writing trenches honing verse structure, building bridges and shaping choruses, I took my demo to virtually every publishing house on the Row, confident with every door that closed, that the next would open.

After ten weeks, I'd been turned down by all but two houses. A week later, all but one.

....

I'd put a lot of stock in pitching myself to Roger Sovine, who was heading up the Welk Music Group at the time. Welk was owned by the legendary Lawrence of the same last name, and was a major player on the Row. Some of the best writers in town were exclusive there, and I'd been able to wrangle a handful of co-writer sessions with several of them: Bob McDill, Dickey Lee, and Jerry Gillespie among them. I was pumped when Roger cleared half an hour for me one afternoon in January. If I couldn't score a draw here, I was going to have to tie a knot at the end of my rope and hang on. Or hang myself.

In Hollywood, screenwriters will tell you—studios will tell you—that if you don't hook the reader by page 10—roughly ten minutes into the film—you never will. A similar rule of thumb exists in popular music: if you don't hook 'em by the tenth bar of the song, they're gone.

Roger handed me a cup of coffee, took my cassette and loaded it into his system.

I'd brought ten tracks; all originals, some co-written, all the best of what I had. He never played one past the tenth bar. A few measures of each song would begin, then his right index finger would shoot up to the fast-forward button, and speed-track through the rest of the tune.

Midway through the tracks, he simply kept his finger poised above the FF button. His face began to change perceptibly in front of my eyes, drooping a fraction of an inch with each song's opening few bars, settling, finally, into what actually looked like anger; that he'd just wasted two and a half minutes of a perfectly good afternoon listening to absolute shit.

'*You're being paranoid*', my other voice whispered sotto voce somewhere behind me, '*These songs have… they've overwhelmed him, man. He literally can't wait to hear what the first few bars of the next song sound like. He's never heard anything like this before. This is your* art. *It's all about to change, man. Be ready.*'

Or something like that.

Roger popped the cassette out of the deck, handed it back to me, and stood.

"Let me ask you a question," he said.

Here it comes. How soon can I be in the studio? What kind of money's it gonna take? Can I have dinner with Hag tomorrow night?

"Have you thought about another career, Buck?"

Wha—what did he just say?

"Maybe something in retail…."

Bile was beginning to rise up from my gut, like magma coursing up through a volcano's pipe. I could barely form comprehensible sounds from my mouth.

"Another…. Something in–*what?*"

"A song plugger, maybe. You've got a great pitch, it's just that—the songs are just—" His office phone rang once, and he grabbed the receiver like it was a life preserver. After a second, he cupped the mouthpiece, turned and smiled.

"I gotta take this. Let's have lunch, man. Maybe next week? I'll have Brenda call you."

He turned back to the phone, stuck his hand out, shook mine and crossed to his desk, his back to me as he sat down.

Cassette in hand, heart on sleeve, I walked the hall back to the lobby like I was moving through wet cement, expecting any second to see a uniformed guard step into the portico at the end of the aisle up ahead and shout, "Dead man walking!…. Dead man walking." I was crestfallen. I could barely roll the joint I'd been hoping to light as a celebration when I got back in the car.

I had no idea how bad it was about to get.

Within an hour after I'd called Murphy and lied to her about the meeting with Sovine *(Went great. He wants to have lunch next week…')* our landlord stopped by to wish us a belated Happy New Year, and to inform us we were two months behind on our rent: a small two-bedroom condo we'd leased from him the year before. We had ten days to pay or thirty to move. Add to that the twenty or so days until Murph went into labor, and it added up to just a wonderful month ahead.

The darkness at the edge of town notwithstanding, the mail that afternoon brought needed relief in the form of an unlooked-for residual check from my short-lived gig as a supporting player on *'Hee-Haw Honeys'*, a shorter-lived CBS series spun off from its namesake. Twenty-four minutes of sketch comedy in a country diner with Misty Rowe, Buck Owens, Roy Clark, Lulu Roman and Gailard Sartain, who was quite possibly among the five funniest people in America. Incredibly, the check was enough to not only cover the rent, but maybe give us a couple hundred buffer.

Life was good. God is great.

On my way to the bank, God set our '76 Pinto on fire and melted every wire and hose under the hood. The engine compartment looked like the inside of an industrial meat smoker. It was too much. Standing on the curb, tears streaming down my face, streets covered in grey slush from the snow the night before, flames licking out from under the Pinto's hood, I raised my fist high in the air, gripping my residual check from Honeys, and shouted heavenward:

"As God is my witness, I *will* be a songwriter! I will *be* a so---"

A loud whump came from somewhere beneath the car, stopping me in mid-soliloquy, and a thick plume of black smoke billowed out from the engine block.

"O.k.….o.k.!," I hollered. "I'll.….I'll look into plugging! *Je*sus!"

With the flames from the block-fire wrapping around it, the right front tire blew, and I did all I could do; said a fitting, pithily elegiac prayer and watched silently as our beloved Pinto dropped to one knee, and died a slow, wheezing, smoky death on the corner of Church and 46th.

I never went into retail.

Of Cornbread Dressing, Gumbo, *and the* Ford Family

Winter 2019

Of Cornbread Dressing, Gumbo, *and the* Ford Family

I AM NOT A SOUTHERNER BY BIRTH; I am a Californian transplanted to the South by way of Colorado. My forty years as a Nashvillian notwithstanding, I confess that half of me still feels inexorably drawn towards The West and the birthplace of my mother; a longing I don't believe any amount of time lived elsewhere will diminish. It is the yin to my yang half, which is pure unadulterated East Tennessee DNA, courtesy my old man. Like the cellular tides within me that physically pull me towards the shores of the Pacific, I confess that I feel a similar, equally strong molecular magnetism when I'm around a pan of sawmill gravy; an iron skillet delicacy I believed for years was a beverage.

As with many families, food was more than just a required staple in our house. It was an integral component of the glue that bound the Fords together. Betty Jean and Ernest Jennings both fancied themselves cut from strong culinary stock, and had the kitchen cred to back it up. But while Betty Jean tended generally towards worldly recipes and dishes beyond the plain Kansan fare of her mother's family, Ernest relied all his life on the traditional food of the south that so clearly informed his youth and shaped his philosophy of the world.

Along the way, both created meals that have flavored my memories not only of them, but of entire swaths of time in our lives together; recollections decades old, made vivid again by aromas, tastes and textures that still whet my appetite as they have for more than half a century.

But of all those scores of recipes, handed-down and made-from-scratch, two remain most prominent in my mind and on my palate; two courses that were far more than merely victuals on the table; they were dishes that all but defined both my mother and my father; heirlooms that will never fade or tarnish. Gifts that in my turn—should God so bless me—that I will hand down to my own children, and perhaps they to theirs.

. . . .

Gumbo has become a term tossed around with so much culinary abandon by so many that call themselves cooks, that, save for a very few examples, the end result never comes even close to accurately describing the very thing it's named for.

Betty Ford, on the other hand, *knew* from gumbo. She knew its roots and ingredients, its histories and its great chefs. With the devotion, dedication, passion (and vodka) of a great artist, she created over time a recipe that became a basic family need, a Cajun-Californian mélange that fed storied entertainers and county jail inmates, alike. A recipe that saw hardened, bitter food critics ripping through their Roget's Thesauri, desperately seeking new adjectives to define and describe what became a signature dish of such gastronomic celebrity that it graced the menus of two of the most legendary Four Star restaurants in history: *Diamond Jim Moran's* in New Orleans, and *Michel's* in Honolulu. Not under the soups and starters, mind you, but under the Entrees; and not merely the name of the dish, mind you, but its creator's, as well; the embossed lettering flourished and elegant, reading simply: BETTY FORD'S CHICKEN GUMBO, giving my mother a kind of fame that, in the annals of great cuisine, anyway, eclipsed even that of her husband's.

. . . .

Ernest Ford's affinity for Southern fare was a thing well-known among all those who knew him; from Presidents to plumbers. As comfortable in the kitchen as was Betty Jean, his true colors as a cook shone brightest during the holidays. He reveled in the preparation, and the anticipation. He could spend hours basting immense turkeys. He ordered enormous hams from a Virginia smoke house weeks before Christmas and had them shipped across the country to friends, admirers, associates and network executives, one of whom had never so much as seen a salt-cured ham covered in mold, let alone been graced with its taste, and promptly, tragically threw it out; a story that, to this date, never fails to bring both groans and laughs equally from those that had.

Like the stock and stoup origins of Betty Ford's Chicken Gumbo, *Ernest Ford's Cornbread and Sausage Dressing* was borne out of his deep and abiding love for his mother and her mastery of one dish; a baked delicacy known across the Clinch Mountains and through the deep wooded vales of East Tennessee with a comestible reputation that transcended even that of her now-famous Applesauce Cake. The simplest of nuanced recipes that experience has taught me people West of the Mississippi will never fully grasp: an iron skillet pan of Southern cornbread.

Humble beginnings, indeed, for a dressing that I try vainly to re-produce each Thanksgiving. A two-day task that begins with that lowly, golden pone and a deep saucepan of turkey broth, seasoned and steeped overnight. Cooled the following morning along with the cornbread, as I cut and dice the greens, and pan fry the smoked and cured pork sausage. Apportioned as I set the oven to 425, grease the baking pan, and begin the mixing, crumbling the corn-bread to a meal-like texture, cutting in the greens and sausage, and slowly, ever so slowly, adding the seasoned broth, to create a texture that glistens with a sheen across its surface as I slowly, ever so slow-ly, pour it into the pan and slide it into the oven. For twenty-two minutes.

. . . .

In truth, calling it simply a *dressing* is woefully short and wide of the mark. Like Betty Ford's Chicken Gumbo, Ernest Ford's Cornbread and Sausage Dressing is, in retrospect, an entire meal, a repast with virtually all the major food groups in one pan. And like Betty Ford's Gumbo, they are meals that have done far more than simply feed me and those at our table. They have sustained me, nourishing both my body and my soul with the memories, histories and love of family that are served with both.

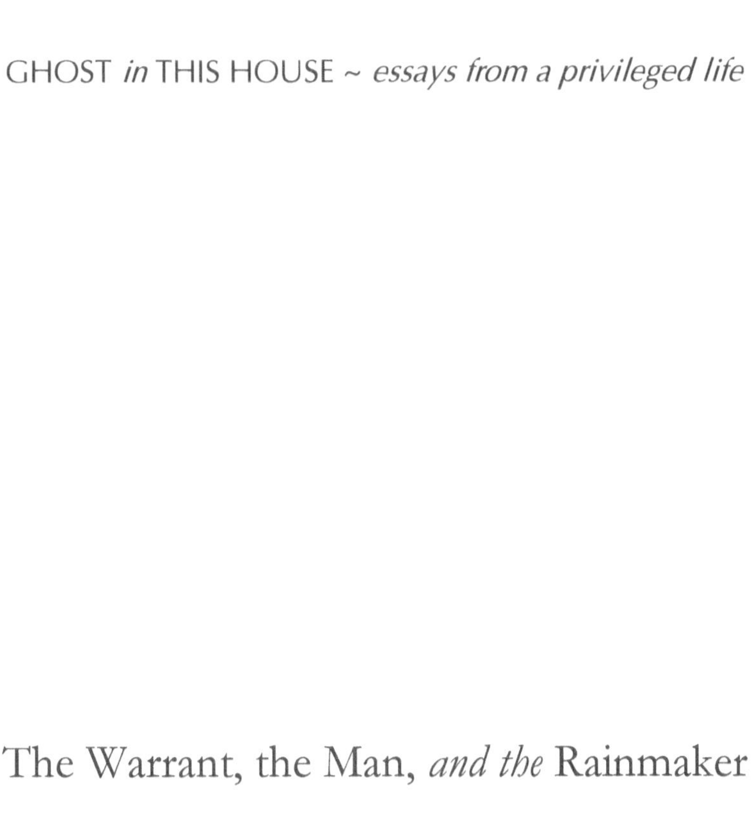

The Warrant, the Man, *and the* Rainmaker

Fall 2021

Circle Tabs 'Rainmaker' Best Play of the Year

By CLARA HIERONYMUS

BEST PLAY of the year honors went to *The Rainmaker*, a comedy drama by N. Richard Nash, at last night's annual meeting of the Circle Players.

It was staged last April with Michael McClen-

Miss McAlister To Become Bride

Mr. and Mrs. Everett S. McAlister of Titusville, Fla., announce the engagement of their daughter, Cynthia Ann, to Philip R. Bowers of Chamblee, Ga., son of Mr. and Mrs. Paul E. Bowers of Morrow, Ga.

The wedding will be July 29.

The bride-elect is a graduate of Valdosta State College where she was a member of Alpha Delta Pi, College Union Board and Cardinal Key, a resident assistant and listed in *Who's Who in American Colleges and Universities*. She is a special education teacher in Atlanta.

don as director and a cast that included James A. Watson, Dallas Cooke, Val Perkins, Wesley Paine, Bill Shick, Bob Tidwell and Wayne Armstrong.

THE PRODUCTION also brought recognition to Wesley Paine as the Best Female Lead for her role as Lizzie Curry, and to Bill Shick as Best non-featured actor.

Lee Green, who has been a stalwart of the Circle (and of Theater Nashville as well) during the past season, was named Best Director for his production of *Two Gentlemen of Verona*.

GREEN AND Jim Goins tied for the theater's most coveted annual prize, the Bauer-Dunlap Award for Outstanding Service to the Circle Theater, and each was given recognition.

Designated Best supporting actor and actress were LaParee Young (*Two Gentlemen of Verona*) and Alice McGeachy (*Blithe Spirit*). Helen Smedley won as best non-featured actress for her work in *Two Gentlemen of Verona*.

PAUL KLAPPER was chosen Best Male Lead for his role in *Harvey*.

Four nominations were made in each of the categories, with selections for top honors made by a critics' panel whose members represent the Nashville community. The awards take the form of engraved silver cups, except for Best Play whose award is an inscribed plaque.

The Warrant, the Man, *and the* Rainmaker

I CAN'T COUNT THE NUMBER OF TIMES I'VE BEEN ASKED how my brief but brilliant career in The Theater began. Mainly because no one ever *has* asked me, per se. But as a multi-hyphenate actor-writer-producer looking through the lens of a life now in the…mid-morning of its autumnal days, I can only hope, only dream of…only imagine that one day—soon—maybe sometime in the next, I don't know, decade, if I'm lucky, some well-meaning soul; a journalist, or a graduate student, perhaps one of my children, composing an essay chronicling scenes from my errant and precipitous life, might pause in their interview, press the REC button on their Voice Memos app and say, "Tell me how your brief but brilliant career in the theater began."

Funny you should ask…

. . . .

By the spring of nineteen and seventy-eight I'd been in Nashville a little less than two years. Murphy and I had been married for close to one of those two, though as I look back now, how or why she stayed even *that* long is quite beyond my reckoning. At twenty-eight I was a veteran bullshit artist, and like all con men of any skill and repute, I'd convinced her I was the best hope we had of climbing out of the snakepit I'd pulled us both into. It's the only explanation that makes any sense.

In that relatively short span of time, I'd managed to have the AMC Pacer I'd driven from Denver repo'd, and Murph evicted from the townhouse she'd lived in for three years. Four months later, in the dead of night, we were skipping out on another, our lives packed and wedged into my brother-in-law's '71 El Camino. In the haste to depart, I made the decision to leave behind a black 27-inch RCA Color Floor Model Television Console I'd acquired from the *Rent-A-Center* on Gallatin Road in Madison, intending to contact one of their always helpful Customer Service Representatives at my earliest free moment while on the lam and provide them the land-lord's telephone number. In hindsight, this proved an unwise course of action on my part; one I learned some days after our flight into the night had me wanted by the *Rent-A-Center* on Gallatin Road in Madison along with the Metropolitan Nashville Police De-partment on a Theft of Rental Property warrant. Putting way too fine an edge on things, I was running an occasional ounce or two of renegade blow to cover our expenses, you know, but I'd been, well…I'd been blowing all the profits and was in the hole a little more than a grand to the… wholesaler.

All of which, when you lined everything up end to end, made for an aspect of newly-married life Murph probably hadn't anticipated.

Events of my own making coursed and colluded around us like a perfect storm of idiocy and bad luck, keeping me running maybe three steps ahead of the law and the man both, and making staying in Twang Town that spring of nineteen and seventy-eight kindly a deal-breaker.

. . . .

We holed up in a rambling old farmhouse in Marshall County with Murph's sister, JoLynn and her husband, Danny; everything we owned packed into a back room and not a dime between us. I took part time labor gigs on construction jobs when Danny's foreman needed another shovel, and borrowed a few hundred scratch from Ernest Ford to keep us alive, but neither was enough to keep the wolf at bay. Jobless, carless, homeless, wanted by the authorities and hiding out from a dental hygienist with an alternate line of income and associates who practiced rearranging teeth, I wasn't yet thirty years old, pregnant with our first child, and by my own hand, staring into the open maw of abject failure.

I desperately needed to make a change, find gainful employment and right the boat. I needed a path, a way to atonement…and I needed about three grand. My credit score was likely being circulated with a mugshot. I'd come to Nashville for the music business, but hadn't booked a gig in months. I had no real training in a hireable skill in the real world and I needed a real world gig—position, rather—something in management, perhaps, something wherein I could capitalize on the skills I *did* possess. Surely someone somewhere needed a moderately talented, part-time entertainer and construction worker with a solid pedigree. Someone practiced in the art of gaslighting. Someone who could convince almost anyone he was someone he wasn't.

When the answer came to me, it came on page three of the Sunday Tennessean's Entertainment section; a small, one color, two-column, four-inch notice buried deep in a printed mosaic of club acts, Opry lineups and Cineplex ads that leapt off the newsprint like on a page in a pop-up book. In the seconds it took me to read, scan and reread this simple rectangular block with a Bold Helvetica headline and eight lines of body copy in Times New Roman 10pt, I knew instinctively that I wasn't merely reading a one color, two-column, four-inch notice buried deep in a printed mosaic of club acts, Opry lineups and Cineplex ads.

I was looking at my destiny, my salvation.

I was looking at a casting call for Community Theater.

The Circle Players, Nashville's preeminent theater troupe and house were auditioning; holding an open call for the Richard Nash staple, *The Rainmaker*. I knew this play, I'd played File when I was boarding in Carmel, what? ten, eleven years earlier? My God, I thought, already putting the plan into gear, if I could land a part in this, all these *I'm-at-the-edge-of-the-abyss-so-get-a-real-fucking-job-now* plans would have to be tabled. For a month at least, maybe two. Money?

I wouldn't make a dime, a couple of hundred dollars at best, but this …this was something I could do. Something I could make. Something I could be.

I dug out an old headshot and resume, wheedled another few hundred in a wire from the old man, and the keys to the El Camino from Danny, and three days later, the big Holley four-barrel wide open, I made the run to town while Murph hung with JoLynn at their Mother and Daddy's.

I couldn't recall the last time I'd auditioned for anything. I'd done a summer season at the Perry-Mansfield Academy after a run as Maitland in *The Glass Menagerie* in Monterey in '68. But that was ages ago, darling. I hadn't trod the boards in years, and wasn't at all sure I could even make the callback cut. I'd checked out a book on American Theater at the library in Lewisburg, and crammed on a condensed version of the play; anything to give me an edge; I was a new kid on the block, Circle vets would be reading; polished, known, marquee names in Nashville theater, and I needed to be firing on all cylinders. I needed to be an actor.

But all the stewing and fretting was for naught. The moment I walked into the theater I knew instinctively I'd leave with a part. Scene after scene, the director released actor after actor, until, at the end of the afternoon, seven of us remained. We'd simply been acquaintances when the day began…new friends. When the auditions ended, we were a cast. Wesley Paine as Lizzie. Wayne Armstrong as

Starbuck. James Watson as HC. Bill Shick as the sheriff. Bob Tidwell as File. Val Perkins as my little brother, Jim and me—Dallas Cooke—as Noah.

Stay with me.

I tore up the stairs when we broke and grabbed a payphone, slugging quarters in to call Murph at her folks', and give her the good news. The next few weeks were going to be frantic, I told her; rehearsals, blocking, wardrobe fittings, set construction…and PR… "They're gonna promote the show the week before opening," I told her. "All three locals and both papers!" I was swelling with pride. I was going to carry on the family name and make my father proud of me at last.

The silence on the phone was so complete, I thought for an instant we'd been disconnected. Then, through the earpiece, the sounds of her family receding, and she, sotto voce:

"What if someone recognizes you?"

Her words froze me with fear. My God, I was going to go to jail and my father would disown me at last. My psyche split into two halves, one, an already-seasoned thespian, positively glowing at the prospect of recognition, the other, a hardened criminal, stricken to mute silence at the prospect of recognition. Then, Murph again, her voice muffled, her hand likely cupping the mouthpiece:

"What if you used a stage name?"

The sheer artfulness, the *genius* of the idea was radiant. My God, this was a brilliant woman. Brilliant and cunning. A *stage* name. It was perfect…and de rigueur for all the most fashionable actors in the theater and the cinema both. I needed something with some brio and panache, something tough and memorable… a man's name, but with a…I don't know…a flair of theatricality.

What I needed was an alias for two months.

The next few weeks, as I'd forecast, were helter-skelter. But God, I felt like I'd been baptized and born again. I'd found a place for myself, and maybe a future for Murph and I. Two talent agents had already come to a handful of rehearsals, and I knew as clearly as I knew my own name—both of them—that I was pinging on their radar. Every rehearsal brought me closer to the character of Noah and to this family; I began to slide into him as effortlessly as it felt to work with this cast; (brilliant) intuitive actors all…and all as panicked and flush as I when I'd learned Dad was going to be in town for a commercial shoot and had bought tickets to opening night for him, his manager, Red Loakes, and my brother, Brion. The news all but cemented me with Circle Players. I was in the gang, now… I was an actor.

As hackneyed and trite as it sounds, I felt like I was home.

Which was where Jerry, the Customer Service Representative from Rent-A-Center who swore the warrant out on me was when Dallas Cooke's headshot came up on his own 27-inch RCA Color Television Console in the local TV ad for the play the night before the curtain rose.

. . . .

On Opening Night, that 'perfect storm of idiocy and bad luck' made landfall at the Circle Theater, arriving in the lobby in the form of two plainclothes detectives, only yards behind Brion, Loakes, and my old man (who, thank God, was completely in the dark), armed with a warrant for my arrest (now including a charge of using an alias to avoid prosecution) and no real taste for legitimate theater.

In the Green Room, we were fifteen minutes from Places when the buzz broke from Dad entering the theater. They'd made it to their seats when Brion muscled his way backstage to wish me luck, and to tell us all how excited he and Dad were to see the show. But he'd only barely opened his mouth when Henry, the stage manager, lurched into the Green Room, his face a kabuki mask of urgency and fear, his hands wringing. "There are two…two men here," he said.

We were five minutes to Places.

In less than three, Brion had absorbed the entire story, told all of us to break a leg, followed Henry out and made his way through the wings and out to the small anteroom where the detectives waited for me. Marching up to both, he extended and shook each of their hands, and introduced himself. Less than two minutes later, he'd convinced them that arresting me before the show was out of the question, and finagled them two seats a few rows behind Dad, who still had no clue.

In the Green Room, the small light blinked on the header above the door, and Henry leaned into the frame. "Places!" he said.

For the next two hours, we mounted a show that would run for four weeks, and be named Best Play of The Year, with Wesley Paine earning Best Actress for the year. Completely beguiled, both detectives became Circle regulars, waited until Ernest Ford left the theater, and allowed me to travel to booking untethered after the doors to the theater had been closed that night.

But when I arrived, I was not alone. I stepped into the precinct to find myself surrounded by my fellow cast members, our Director, Michael McClendon, our stage manager, Henry, and the Circle's resident attorney, all there linking hands for Dallas; Dallas Cooke.

After some maneuvering, both charges were eventually resolved and the record of both cleared from my file. It took a little more tap dancing, but eventually I covered the contraband nut—with interest.

Ernest Ford? Never had a clue.

And that, dear reader, was the *real* theater.

Venda, the Caprice, *and the* Martini

Summer 2018

Venda, the Caprice, *and the* Martini

BETWEEN THE FALL OF EIGHTY-FIVE and the spring of ninety-nine, I hit a fairly decent stride as fairly busy C-List supporting actor. Seven television series, a couple of national commercials, and fourteen films. Throw in a handful of legit theatre things, and it comes to twenty some-odd credits in fourteen years and change. Not a bad run considering I was based out of Nashville; not a town noted for its thriving thespian community. Had family, the law, betrayal, and tragedy not intervened, I might be writing this from my trailer on location in some far-flung corner of the country.

George Burns is down somewhere as saying something like, *'Acting is all about honesty. If you can fake that, you've got it made.'* Truth. I wasn't a real versatile actor; I was a lucky actor. I tended to essentially play the same guy regardless of what I was reading for: myself. Myself, but with just enough authority to make my character a necessary cog in the story; a slimy, disreputable and morally vacant cog, normally, but necessary nonetheless. I found a commonality with these characters; smallish men who felt a need to exercise that authority, to draw that sword. It came easy for me to slip these characters on, too easy, maybe. But I was getting the work—what are you gonna do?

But that's not the point of this story. The point of this story is murder.

. . . .

In the summer of nineteen and ninety-eight, I killed an extra on the set of a picture I was less than a day away from wrapping in South Africa. It was a terrible thing, I'll grant you; a moment I still deeply regret. But a moment that was not altogether unforeseen. She had a rep for being difficult on the set, thought she ruled the roost around the other extras, and was known to use heavily when she was working. Hard stuff. Word around the studios was it was just a matter of time before she bought it. That she was strung out that day and couldn't walk a straight line didn't really matter. That I maybe bore some of the fault didn't really matter. Killing her, though, put the shooting sked behind by more than two hours. And in the movie business, that mattered.

The story circulated for weeks after the wrap...months, really, and I replayed the accident again and again in my mind's eye for just as long or longer. Mainly because no one who was on the set that day let me forget it. It followed me off location like a cur at my heels and hung about my neck like an albatross. For years, extras wranglers on every picture I worked on made it a point to herd their talent away from me. It was humiliating.

Then, after five, maybe six years of not hearing a single peep, I thought the tale had finally run its course. But when a grip that worked the picture told the story at a cocktail party not long ago, it all came back like a bad flashback, albeit with an extra added attraction: not only had it not dried up and blown away over those six years like I'd hoped—it had survived, it had taken on a life of its own, and become a kind of C-movie legend, a straight-to-video urban myth grown so fat with added scenes and so flocked with garnishment that even I had trouble recognizing it.

Certain I'd never be able to show my face in Burbank again, I fled the party; every guest, it seemed, clucking and laughing at me behind their hands as I passed their tables.

"It's time," my agent said across the telephone line one late afternoon not long after. "The bloody thing's only going to keep...*living*, for God's sake. Unless you do something."

She's right, I thought, as I pressed the small END button on the keypad. It was time. Time to free myself at last from the memory, the stigma, and the guilt.

It was time, once and for all, to tell the truth. To tell the real story of what happened that day.

The day Venda Kruger was killed.

. . . .

The outlands north and east of Cape Town could've passed for Kansas. South Dakota, maybe. Vast stretches of wheat and maize patchworked among broad, fenced fields of barley and sorghum.

Droves of sheep grazed lazily in the grasslands along both sides of the road, their backs like woolen whitecaps bobbing atop verdant, open waters. Across the plains, great hulking grain mills stood here and there like giant Burning Man sculptures, with golden halos of chaff dust rising from their silo caps.

We were a good half hour from the set for that day, a working farm built from the ground up by the production carpenters in just over a month. Four-stall barn, outbuildings...sheds and coops, and a two-story log home with bleached tin roofing and a thirty-foot long porch anchoring the front face. Sweeping fields of waist-high wheat surrounded it all, stretching for acres in all directions, giving the farm the appearance of an island, a floating oasis anchored in a flaxen sea.

It was our third day there, and the final day of a 62-day shoot. A film launched under an ill-fated banner from the start and doomed to a shelf-life shorter than a can of Spam. A *Home Alone-meets-Treasure Island-meets-Time Tunnel* mashup family comedy adventure that promised to be a breakout of sorts for its lead, Jim Varney, until he lost the role to a cancer diagnosis and Tim Curry before the first table read. A film that very nearly cost director John Cherry every dime he had, and co-star Charlie Napier his life. A film that found me retching in a service alley behind the hotel at half-past eleven one night, after being hypnotized by Dee Wallace Stone. A film we all knew was going straight to Blockbuster but we all had our reasons for doing. A film that threw us all together in the most unlikely of places, and challenged us to get out…alive. I, for one, was anticipating an eventful, but bittersweet last day, looking forward to the wrap party and hoping that the varmint wranglers had cleared the trailers and loos of snakes and spiders. And the beetles. The goddamned *beetles*…..

I slid the sides for the day out of my shoulder bag and turned on the van's dome lamp, careful that I not awaken Dee, her head resting gently on my jacketed shoulder. At the top in bold caps, the title and logline stretched across the page header:

PIRATES OF THE PLAIN
Adventure Beyond Their Wildest Dreams

But my hope of not awakening her was all too short-lived. I'd only just begun scanning my lines when the van rounded a bend, lurched violently from one side of the highway to the other and came to a screeching halt in the middle of the road, throwing us all against the straps of our seatbelts, and whiplashing us to our seat backs like a vanfull of crash-test dummies.

For a chaotic moment, we all checked one another, our eyes searching each of us for signs of any injury. Until one-by-one, our gazes were pulled to the windscreen, the scene outside the van almost too surreal to acknowledge.

You've seen the films or stills a hundred times; a narrow road in Scotland or Colorado and a car literally surrounded by a herd of livestock; sheep or cows, all content to meander just as slow as they please while the driver barely inches forward.

This was like that. But different. We were surrounded, alright, but not by livestock. No genial old herder rode or walked behind this ambling mass.

Slivers of sunlight cut through the van's windows, the first fingers of dawn just curling over the rim of Howequas Mountain to the east. Had it been any earlier, we might not've seen them. We might've plowed right into them. And as many as were there, it's likely one or more of us might've been killed.

Their species is called *Papio Ursinus*. One of the more social of their kind, highly intelligent, known to grow as large as humans and travel in great numbers or *troops*. To many people in this part of the world, they're called the Chacma. But to most in the veldt north of Cape Town they're simply called the Cape Baboon. And right now, we were encircled by scores of them. Great hairy beasts, loping across the road with their red asses held aloft and murder in their eyes.

For a moment, we were all too stunned to speak...and perhaps too frightened; that the sound of any one of us saying even one word might draw them towards us. Slowly, I scanned the interior, thinking, I'm riding to the set of a barely-breathing movie in a '92 Toyota microbus with Tim Curry, Dee Wallace Stone, and Charlie Napier. It's 5:15 in the morning, there's no coffee in the van, Napier's hung over, there's a troop of baboons as big as men surrounding the van. And we're in the middle of South Africa.

What else could possibly go wrong?

....

We found out what else could possibly go wrong at 3:18 that afternoon.

The last day of principal photography on a picture is beautiful thing. There is a sense of...conclusion. Of accomplishment. Of closure. It informs virtually everyone and every minute on the set and propels the team towards a finish line that looms nearer by the minute; a finish line marked ceremoniously, reverently, even, on some pictures, with The Last Shot of the Last Day. A shot so anticipated, so beloved, so important, that it was given its own entry in the great lexicon of film terminology. A cinematic sobriquet of such conclusive power that when heard or spoken could reduce even the most hardened of production veterans to tears. A shot traditionally called out by the 1st AD, or the production manager; called out from the camera line with a bullhorn, the AD's voice blaring across the set with the revelatory zeal of a barrelman high atop a crow's nest sighting land. At 2:45 Patrice Leung brought the megaphone she kept holstered on her right hip to her mouth and hit the TALK button.

"MARTINI SHOT IS UP!" she bellowed.

Around the great log home, some seventy people erupted into

spontaneous, prolonged applause, then turned their eyes, their attention, and, yes, their hopes, to me.

The Martini, you see, was mine. An honor normally reserved for everything from the simplest of coverage shots to final shots of the lead....but a privilege I'd never held in twenty years of making films.

The setup was unremarkable...elementary, really. Bent on swindling Dee, her father (Charlie) and her son (Seth Adkins) out of their family farm, I'd come to discuss 'terms' with Dee. I pull through the gate, up to the house, step out of the car, and into a fertilized gift from one of the cows created just for me by the crack team in the special effects trailer. Three cameras: one on a crane to follow the car through the gate.

With a walkie-talkie on the passenger seat to relay direction from John, I climbed into my picture car: a nineteen-ninety dark blue Caprice Classic. Soft tricot-cloth interior, ribbed to look like hand-stitching. Power seats and windows. Cold air.

We rehearsed the scene four times: twice for timing, and twice for angles and lighting. It was a snap. This was literally a no-brainer.

The walkie-talkie burped to life next to me. Patrice:

"Ok...settle, please. Buck, hold. Annnddd....Extras in."

From the back of the house a pickup appeared. An older model Toyota with a five-foot tall stock rack squaring the bed and containing three long wooden cages stacked three high. From behind my Ray-Bans, behind the wheel of the Caprice, I watched as the wrangler, Ethan Kruger, a weathered and storied Afrikaner known by every film crew on the continent, got out of the cab, walked around to the back of the SR5, dropped the tailgate, opened the latches on all three wooden cages, and two-by-two, brought out the extras for the Martini shot.

Fifteen South African chickens.

Fifteen mildly tranquilized South African chickens.

For what seemed an eternity, Ethan Kruger carefully moved hens and roosters from the truck to the ground, placing each upon their mark. Beautiful birds, all. Ovambo bantams and free-range Koekoeks. Naked Neck roosters and a duo of Rhode Island Reds. All obviously precious to Ethan... his moneymakers, yes, but his children in almost all respects, evinced not only in the gentleness with which he handled each bird, but in the fact that each had a given first name and Ethan's own surname. With the driver's side window powered down even slightly, I could hear the old man talking quietly to each bird.... his voice rising and falling among their clucks and peeps.

With the brood milling about his feet, Ethan turned one last time to the open cages, reached in to the topmost pen, and withdrew the last extra. A massive bird, nearly as big as a goose. A bird that carried no small amount of baggage with her. A rumored prima donna with four pictures to her credit, including *'Cry the Beloved Country'* in ninety-five with Charlie Dutton and Richard Harris.

The cast and crew all took in an audible breath as Ethan turned, his beloved Venda resting in the cradle of his arms, her brilliant plumage of black and white and red glistening under the waning light of the westering South African sun. He no sooner placed her on the ground with the others than she began earning her rep, establishing her own pecking order, as it were, nipping at every other bird near her until she'd created a buffer between her and them.

The bit was simple: Ethan slowly herds the birds to the drive, then, out of frame, waves a brightly painted piece of cardboard the birds know, scattering them as I pull in. Chickens mildly tranc'ed, me driving at about 2 mph...nobody saw a problem.

On the seat beside me, the walkie-talkie burped to life again: Patrice.

"Ok... everybody settle, please. This is for the martini.... in 3...2... Ethan: extras..... and Buck... action."

I slid the Caprice into D, turned through the gate and into the drive, my ears tuned to the walkie-talkie and my eyes glued to my stop-mark ahead. To my left, Ethan was waving the brightly painted cardboard and all the chickens were scattering across the drive on cue.

The first instinct I had that something was amiss was the slight, very nearly imperceptible rise-and-fall of the right front end of the car, followed by the same sensation from the right rear. I remembered neither from the four rehearsals, and wondered how I'd missed the clod I'd obviously just driven over.

The next instinct I had was that my first instinct was wrong. Way, way wrong. Off to my left, old Ethan Kruger was loping as fast as he could towards the Caprice, tears welling in his eyes. Beside me, the walkie-talkie again came to life, but the voice now was the director's. Even through the static, I could make out the unmistakable sound of John Cherry exhaling before he spoke even one word...

"Oh, man..." he sighed. To my right, now, Ethan disappeared below the door-frame of the Chevy. As he slowly rose into view, John came back on the radio, telling me what I already knew.

"Ok... let's, um, let's cut, man. You, um.....you just, uh...." but from the open passenger window, Ethan finished for John:

"You *bastard*. You just killed my Venda."

. . . .

I was, of course, exonerated, and eventually even old Ethan apologized and acknowledged as much, but for the rest of the day, the death wore heavily on us all, placing a decidedly pitty olive in what should've been a fabulous martini. Packed back into the microbus, the long ride back to Cape Town and the hotel after the wrap was like being in a sensory-deprivation chamber; my cast-mates all but shunning me. It was mortifying.

Against my better judgement, I listened to Dee, Charlie and Tim and went to the wrap party, where we screened dailies and I drank myself into near-forgetfulness, regretting the pending separation from the cast and crew and hoping that the memory of the day's accident had faded from their minds as well. Sufficiently oiled with a serious South African Merlot, I was gathering myself up to return to my room when Tim and Dee sidled up to me with a dinner invitation to join them in Charlie's room in an hour. Having done no more than pick at finger food for as long, I jumped at it, taking a detour to my room where I splashed some water on my face, changed clothes, grabbed another bottle of wine, and at seven-thirty, made my way to Napier's room.

I'd barely knocked when Dee opened the door, gave me a quick peck on the cheek, and led me into the suite, where Charlie, Tim, and John waited for me at the dining table, beautifully set with white bone china, silver and crystal surrounding the meal my friends... my dear, dear friends... had prepared for me, catered from the newest fast-food enterprise in Cape Town.

A bucket of KFC.

Straightman

Fall 2014

Straightman

IN THE SPRING OF 2009, EXILED FROM HOME and family and lost in Paradise, I could not have known that my long road back to the land of the living would lay one-hundred twenty miles to the south, deep in the desert, and would begin when I quit L.A., walked away from the business, and became the live-in caregiver for a dying, legendary queen of Old Hollywood and Palm Springs.

My Uncle.

That he wasn't actually my real uncle, and wasn't really a …*queen-*queen, as defined by those who…. define those things, is beside the point. He'd have loved the line—loved the fact that anything at all was being written about him.

. . . .

James Leroy 'Red' Loakes was a man Lee Liberace once dubbed *"the best-known* unknown *man in show business"*. As Dad's personal manager, he was a fixture in his career and in our family for nearly fifty years. Trusted friend, loyal confidante, understanding big brother, and aide-de-camp rolled into one. A man I'd known from my earliest memory as simply Uncle Red. A man many of the most powerful people in Hollywood called. *The Last of the Great Major-*

domos. But south of L.A., along the sun washed boulevards and adobe-lined streets of Palm Springs, he was known by his long-time consorts in the Rainbow Posse as Pops; a sobriquet from a life he'd struggled for decades to keep safely hidden in the shadows of the closet. A closet that, by the end of 2009, was holding more than three million gay and grey senior citizens in the United States alone; a burgeoning group AARP and Newsweek called an "invisible and overlooked" segment of our population; one in which many of its millions of members still lived with one foot in the shadows of that closet -- seniors who spent years hiding their sexuality, and living in secrecy. The generation that produced Rock Hudson and Liberace, that witnessed Stonewall, knew that their lives and careers, and possibly those of the people they were closest to, depended on that secrecy. For Loakes, it meant not just hiding who and what he was, but cultivating every outward appearance to the belief that he wasn't. In the posse's enclaves, Red Loakes was the straightest gay man among them. The running gag was, he was so straight he had corners.

It was a defense mechanism he guarded viciously, and honed fearfully. In the social and political climate of the fifties through the very early sixties, had the world learned then that the man closest to of one of the most iconic, beloved entertainers of the age was gay, it would have been nothing short of social and professional murder-suicide. Sensationalism doesn't come close to describing what the

AP and UPI, TV Life, and every rag from Phoenix to Philadelphia would have done with this story. It would have been yellow press run amok. It would have gone viral when the word meant something completely different.

Red Loakes - trusted aide and confidante – the man who'd spent his entire life managing the lives of others – had somehow managed for half a century to lead two. But now, living alone, approaching eighty, his health rapidly failing, Mr. Last of the Great Majordomos was having trouble managing either one.

He needed new material. The network wasn't renewing. The curtain was coming down.

He was dying.

He needed help. He needed a cook, a nurse, a driver, a house-keeper…a companion. He needed a caregiver; somebody stable, dependable… somebody not carrying any baggage.

I took the gig anyway.

. . . .

This is not an essay about caregiving. I have neither the credentials nor the expertise to write knowledgeably about the subject, and my experience is limited to only one charge. Like ninety percent of the eighteen million whose ranks I briefly joined, I didn't believe I had a choice in the matter. I know, of course, that I did; I could have politely left the medical intervention under a believable ruse, made it completely legitimate in his eyes by tying it somehow to the business, and gone back to L.A.

I could have simply declined. Declined, taken fringe interest when he was eventually placed somewhere, said something fitting at his funeral, and buried a lifetime of memories both bright and dark with him. I could have simply declined and turned away from this man who was the face and voice of those memories; who was the last link in the chain that had encircled me for my entire life, and who, despite all, had spent his own life in service to our family.

I chose otherwise.

Encouraged by his doctors and those closest to him, advised and believing in my heart that his death was imminent, I closed down the apartment in Brentwood, booked out indefinitely from my agents in Hollywood, and took a spare bedroom in his Palm Springs condo, expecting I'd be out of the loop and off the grid for a couple of months at best.

I was wrong on that one.

Seven months later, I was able to identify some fifteen tablets and capsules by sight. WebMD was bookmarked on both my laptops and my Blackberry. I could bathe and dress a two-hundred eighty pound man in ten minutes and was breaking land-speed records rotating bladder bags in less than sixty seconds. I could navigate my way through every wing in two hospitals and every outpatient clinic between La Quinta and Rancho Mirage, and had the clearance to perform CPR in three.

I was caregiving, people. You lead, you follow, or you get out of the way.

A year later, I was literally living a sitcom pitch. Seriously.....

Take one socially liberated, but sexually secure emotional refugee from Tennessee, with a thirty-year marriage drifting on and off the rocks and a career headed for the ditch, and quarantine him for eighteen months in the desert of Palm Springs, California, with an ailing and afflicted gay octogenarian, slowly drifting in and out of dementia. Add a supporting ensemble of Medicare's Finest, a troupe of neighbors straight out of Central Casting, a bronzed clique of show business dinosaurs, and a well-meaning, but drama-prone posse of old-school boys from San Francisco and you've got this year's must watch newest comedy. It's Bill Murray and Paul Giamatti together – in stories that will warm your heart…. Stories of acceptance and surrender, life and death – and of two older men of the opposite sex living together.

Straightman – tonight at 9 -- 8 Central.

Had I listened to a handful of well-meaning souls, I'd have been blogging about it every day, like the Julie and Julia thing, or the Waiter Rant guy. But I'd have been the *Clinically-Depressed-Live-in-Straight-Caregiver-For-the-Gay-Octogenarian* guy. Inserted incognito into the sordid and tawdry underworld of the gay senior citizen. In the sordid and tawdry desert resort of Palm Springs. Biting and riveting reportage from the caregiving trenches. Live Facebook updates from the urology lab, and YouTube uploads from the cocktail terrace afterwards. Special Editions, perhaps, on how to humbly accept the honor of returning the favor for someone who once changed *your* diaper. Or, what to say and/or do when the elderly gay gentlemen you're bathing is…*happy* to see you.

I didn't think it had legs, but there you go.

. . . .

Despite all empirical evidence to the contrary, I suspect there will be a number of people, perhaps some that I am acquainted with, who will read this story, possibly only thus far, and immediately assume that they were right all along. That I'm gay.

I'm not.

Seriously. I'm not.

I am, I'll admit, a little gay*ish*, I suppose. Well, post-gayish, with a few lingering wardrobe manifestations. And I owe it all to science.

Stay with me.

There is, I have learned, a socio-scientific phenomenon referred to as *attributive cultural reflection*, or, *culture absorption*; a 'common social defense mechanism' that usually kicks in with cases of people from one part of the world spending a long period of time in a completely different part of the world. The language, customs, and practices are wholly foreign to them—in every way, shape and form they are strangers in a strange land. Adapt and adopt become the operative words. You want to blend in, not stick out. You shop and eat where the locals do. You wear the uniform. You hang with the homeys. In time, you begin to reflect the cultural attributes you've absorbed. You begin to take on the mannerisms, the gait and the cadence of the environment you're in. It's a matter of social survival. Take somebody from South Philly, maybe, or Boston, and drop him in, say, The Clinch Mountains in East Tennessee for a couple of years. Dollar to a doughnut he comes out saying *y'all* and wanting to know if he can have gravy with that.

Now, you take the same guy, same two years, but drop him in Palm Springs -- doesn't matter where he's from, what he does, how much of a hetero man's man he is—you turn just a *liiiittle* gay. You start thinking about fabrics that won't stick to your back in the summer and tickets for Chorus Line. You start calling everyone honey and you make notes of cosmetic surgery discounts you see in the local paper. You begin wondering aloud about eye lifts and asking strangers if that's a Tommy Bahama they're wearing.

You're *gayish*, honey. It's osmosis. After six months, I looked at it as training. I'm an actor, you know. Training is important. And for God's sake, you know it's paying off when you get hit on by more old white guys in a year and a half than all the women that ever even looked at you sideways your entire life.

In time, the posse would just laugh and wave off the interlopers that didn't know me.

"Don't waste your time, honey", they'd say through a drink . He's a straightman."

I cannot claim to have been a caregiver for those eighteen months in the truest sense of the word. I am in awe of those that have made it their careers – their lives. People cut from a cloth far stronger than my own. Humble, giving souls. Selfless to a fault. The well-being of others the compass that guides them. In that last, most important of attributes, I failed the task, performing it daily not for whatever good it was doing for my charge but more for my own selfish reasons. As time progressed, I became conscious that it was my own well-being that was being served.

When I finally began the process of setting the memory of those eighteen months down on paper, I realized, looking back upon the journey, that I was not only writing a caregiver's chronicle of the last days of one man's life, but a record of the first days of another's. A story of fate and an unlikely partnership. Of loyalty, family, and love. Of two lifelong friends on a journey only one would finish. An account of the redemptive power that the daily -- the *hourly* business of doing for another can generate in one's life. And how, for this author, it became an unyielding weapon in cutting through the bonds of an overwhelming grief and the darkness of depression. It was losing its control; losing its grip and lifting. Losing its strength because I was no longer empowering it; no longer focusing on the battles I was fighting within myself, but on those of another, who could no longer fight for himself.

. . . .

I stand quietly, knowing he will sense me soon enough and rouse from nodding, but he doesn't stir. Beyond the weak lift-and-drop *of his chest, he is completely still. Should one of these ragged intakes turn out to be his dying breath, I know in my heart he would want to breathe it where he was now, here, in this office, his sanctuary. He would want to be surrounded, as he was now, by unfinished work, files open and incomplete, schedules unfinished and unmapped, the squares in the blotter calendar vacant save for thin scratchings from one of the Ticonderoga No.2's he keeps lethally sharp.*

In the half-light cutting into the room through the window shades, I am tuned to his breathing. I listen for its rhythms and tones, and watch for its depth and its form. On the longest days, I watch for the rise and fall of the orchids on the front of his aloha shirt, expecting and prepared for each weakening breath to be his last. With every thin intake and reedy exhale, the faded indigo and plum petals resting at the center of his chest move like time-lapse footage; curling inward and closing upon themselves, lying still and motionless in the concave of that cavity for what seems far too long, then opening briefly, reaching for the thin bands of diffused sunlight filtering through the blinds before curling inward and folding closed again.

Wheels

Fall 2017

Wheels

I WAS BORN AND BAPTIZED A METHODIST to a father of like faith and a mother of lapsed Catholicism... with a marked tendency to vodka. Like most of the hard-shell Baptist, relocated Southern Episcopalian, 'go cut a switch' Presbyterian lessons impressed upon me as a youth, I never truly understood the meaning, let alone the importance, of what it is to bear witness. It suggests a much narrower gap between science and religion that Psychology Today and the Catholic Church—Christianity as a whole, really—both offer the same essential definition: *'to make a solemn statement or affirmation of a thing or event; to share the story of a thing that took place or a word that was spoken. To offer evidence. Worthy, true evidence.'*

Now, I am neither a clinician nor a cleric, and I don't presume to offer this piece of narrative evidence, worthy or not, as either. Beyond twenty-five years on the fringes of the advertising business, I have no knowledge or schooling of any kind in the field of psychology and cannot speak to it in any fashion. As for the latter... well, as for the latter, while I was raised under a Christian roof, and still regard myself as such, I must also confess that I am not a man driven by or wholly adherent to the faith. I do not claim membership among any congregation and I eschew the trappings and condescension of Sunday Christians. I do not end my outgoing message with the hope that whoever's calling me will *have a blessed day.* I do not pray before the decisions I make or the meals I eat and I do not look for the hand of God in my daily business.

But here is the thing.... the thing I have wrestled with and dreamt of. The thing that has claimed so much of my waking thought for the past year, now. The thing that has compelled me...*driven* me to put this pen to paper.

I believe I have seen it.

I believe I have seen the whorls of that Hand's imprint. I believe I have witnessed the evidence of it, the proof of its work. Moreover, I believe I have seen that proof in the eyes of nine women. Nine women I believe—nine women I *know*—were touched by that Hand.

And here's the other thing. The thing that kindly throws a hitch in the whole getalong. The thing that pitches a little clod in the churn.

I witnessed it on a used car lot.

. . . .

For eighteen months I'd had the distinct and altogether humbling honor of directing the philanthropy effort for that used car company--a small, niche-market outfit in Franklin, Tennessee that will, for various reasons, go unnamed. A company that had broken every stereotype of the business, by literally basing their business on one simple philosophy.

The act of giving.

In just over five years, that philosophy drove them to give away forty nearly-new cars to hard-hit women and families in Nashville, in concert with their partners at Thistle Farms, Safe Haven Family Shelter, End Slavery Tennessee and Mercy Multiplied...four houses of refuge staffed by heroes. Heroes whose greatest power and strength is that of simple compassion.

While it's technically and professionally accurate that I was on the giving, business end of things in nine of those forty cases, I would be lying if I left it at that. And lying is a.... you know.

The truth is, after directing the second of those nine Gives, it became something of an addiction for me...a wholly selfish act on my part. Each successive Give an attempt...a prayer, that I might recapture what I believed I had seen in its predecessor event; what I believed I had witnessed in the eyes and upon the faces of each of the women who came before. Women who had come from lives so shattered, so fraught with fear and loss, and so far beyond the shade, to be removed from any reality we might conjure up in our darkest imaginations.

The thing I believed I'd witnessed, you see... the thing I believed I'd seen in their eyes was hope. But a hope so palpable, so overwhelming, that it threatened to envelop not just each of these nine women, but all those surrounding them. A hope gripping each of them so powerfully that it seemed to leave an imprint upon them....

as if they'd been lifted up, and held fast by a great hand.

But it was the knowledge of what sparked that hope, what gave rise to it and illuminated it that I write about now. A thing that I, and most, if not all of you reading this, take for granted so completely that the idea of living our lives without it—without them—is almost impossible to imagine.

Wheels.

. . . .

Over those eighteen months, I'd seen and photographed so many automobiles that they'd all begun to run together. It took something real special to move me past seeing nothing but steel and rubber and chrome and glass.

But to each of the nine women I stood beside at the very moment of the reveal of their new ride, it was clear that they were seeing something else. Something much more than four wheels. They were seeing a road. A map. And a key. They were seeing the journey they were on opening up before them.

They were seeing the hope of freedom.

. . . .

I have lived a long and charmed life. I have traveled to far ports in the world, and stood upon its stages. I have worked alongside Oscar winners and spoken with Presidents. I have been blessed beyond measure and seen wonders beyond reckoning.

But all of it pales and fades into the mist of memory when I look back on the faces of those nine women, clear now, and present in my thought. Nine women whose faces, etched into my mind and heart, are the only evidence I have with which to bear this witness. Nine women I was privileged to stand beside in a moment in time when, regardless of how far I might've drifted from the faith of my fathers, I believed that we were all touched by that great and powerful Hand. Nine singular moments on a used car lot when my life changed. Forever.

Swear to God.

The Old Man *and the* Season

Winter 2017

The Old Man *and the* Season

THERE WAS A TIME, NOT ALL THAT LONG AGO, when I loved the Holidays more than any time of year. The moment the air felt like fall, visions of pumpkin pie would dance in my head; leaves brilliant with colors falling like petals from a sky scented with elm and oak fires burning in warm homes filled with families. Halloween was the opening act for Thanksgiving, and the day after Thanksgiving, the search for The Tree would begin.

For years, I labored selfishly under the assumption that my own family; my children and my wife, felt the same; that they looked forward with the same hope and anticipation as I. I assumed that the traditions of both our families—my wife's and mine—would carry over to ours, taking from both, and creating our own Holiday traditions; sacred recipes long-held secret, taken out only once a year and placed on the table with the reverence of sacraments. Ornaments from generations before, each with a memory and a story attached, unwrapped as if rare jewels, and hung side-by-side with clay and felt decorations made in kindergarten.

For two months, hope, tradition, and promise were side-by-side with abundant tables and family. I would begin and end each day praying that our sons and our daughter would carry the traditions forward... forward and into the folds of their own families in the years to come.

I know now that nothing of what I'd hoped was ever present in them; that they did not share the same sense of spirit and tradition that I did. I know now that by devoting myself–for even two months—to the trappings of the past and the bindings of family, that I was hanging my own Holiday culture of what I believed a family should be on them. Like an ornament.

I know now that I was wrong about all of it, and that I may have tarnished whatever good they may have had in their hearts once, or ever would, for those two days, for this season.

. . . .

And so, this year, as the last, and the years before, I will not mark these days as I once did. I will not awaken with carols on the radio, or rejoice at the sight of a pan of perfect cornbread. I will not fly through the mall searching for the one gift I know will please, nor ply through the rows of fir and spruce and pine for the tree that might have been our Center. I will not lie awake in the days and weeks before, barely able to contain my anticipation.

This year, as the last, and the years before, I will hold it all in my own heart, and keep my own counsel. I will not harden my children's hearts with my own selfishness over traditions, hopes, dreams and ... two days in a season that only mattered to me.   This year, as the last, and the years before, I will hope and I will pray; for peace in their lives, and that they might one day forgive an old man who was too blind to see, too deaf to hear, and lost in his own way.

The Wasteland

Fall 1999

The Wasteland

I WAS BORN INTO, AND RAISED IN THE CULTURE of television. It was an integral part of the family business. I literally grew up with it. In those years, network television offered us three, maybe four channels... five if you counted NET (PBS's predecessor). We planned our weeknights as a family around what was on. You could count the number of great prime time shows on two hands, and still have one or two fingers left.

Today, there are roughly 300 channels on most cable boxes. And nothing's on. Unless you count reality TV. And here's the count: in 2018, 273 reality shows debuted or renewed. Two. Hundred. Seventy. Three. Sixty-three scripted shows debuted or renewed the same September. Sixty-three.

The 'reality' is, we have become a nation of voyeurs, obsessed with the lives of people who have no business exposing their lives to us, and moreover, should be ashamed that they've allowed those lives to become the fodder of our entertainment' The "stars" of most of these shows are borderline illiterate, socially itinerant idiots. But our culture has elevated them to the strata of Celebrity.

We... *celebrate* them.

We celebrate their tawdriness, their ignorance of basic grammar and the English language. We know what they ate for breakfast and who had breast augmentation. We cheer grown women whose careers depend on how wealthy and cruel they can be, and we applaud men whose intelligence quotients are measured by the circumference of their arms, or the length of their…. beards. We create spinoffs of the more appealing idiots, and talk shows hosting the most vile. We wait with baited breath in front of the flat screen for the insults, base behavior and cheap wardrobe we know are imminent.

The great experiment, the storyteller, the babysitter…. the console that once carried us away to The Ponderosa, took us aflight on The Enterprise, made the Ricardos and the Bunkers and the Cosbys our own families has become nothing more than a peepshow; a tarnished nickelodeon you wash your hands after using, its fading light flickering in the back room of the Arcade once known as America.

I gotta go. Naked Amish Afraid of the Mafia is on.

The Lesson, the Klan, *and the*
Old Rugged Cross

Fall, 2022

22 Oneonta Star   Wed., Sept. 22, 1965

They play his song

Ernie protests to KKK

By Dorothy Kilgallen

Tennessee Ernie Ford has written a letter of protest to the Ku Klux Klan because the Kluxers have been playing Ernie's recording of "The Old Rugged Cross" at their meetings and burnings. Lots of luck, Ernie, but the Klan doesn't pay any attention to the Chief Justice of the United States, or the Attorney General, or the President; they're hardly likely to be upset by a note from a singer.

Dorothy Kilgallen story....
Sept. '65

The Lesson, the Klan,
and the Old Rugged Cross

I DON'T KNOW IF MY FATHER was what you'd call a brave man. I'd like to think he was, but I suppose there are many sons or daughters who would like to think the same of their own father. He was principled to a fault, resolute in his beliefs, and steadfastly held to the lessons taught him as a child. Lessons he hoped and strove to pass on to my brother and I. Lessons rooted in the traditions and histories of his faith and his forebears; lessons he prayed would shape our character and define how we lived our lives among others; their simplicity the key to the enduring value each held: tell the truth. Earn your way. Respect your elders. Don't take it if it isn't yours. And his mother's worn old saw: *Don't judge a book by its cover or a man by his color.*

In the South, in the time of Ernest Ford's youth, that last lesson, while preached quietly in the churches and meeting places of his people, was not one practiced, shared or observed by the congregants at large. Bristol, Tennessee, like hundreds of cities and towns below and above the Mason-Dixon Line was divided along borders of black and white, and rarely did the twain meet or cross those lines; lines defined not only by color, but by faith, origin, poverty and fear. Lines controlled, patrolled and ridden by respected members of the community; men Clarence, Maude, Stanley and Ernest Ford all knew well. Men Clarence worked alongside, and went to church with; men who ran businesses, worked in slaughterhouses, delivered mail, held political office, and taught school. Men who also kept a second, secret identity, one hidden under embroidered and patched sheets they wore with white hoods over their heads.

In the South, in the time of Ernest Ford's youth, the Ku Klux Klan was as common a fixture of the socio-fraternal landscape as the Masons or the Odd Fellows. Imperial knights of Christendom they portrayed themselves, sworn in secret rituals to protect and defend the soil, blood and honor of America from the great hordes of all those who were unwashed in the Protestant blood. To speak against them publicly was to bring scorn upon your name and reputation, and brought into question your patriotism. To associate with those they were sworn to rid America of was to invite mockery, exclusion and perhaps even violence upon one's home and family.

But to Clarence and Maude Ford, in the years of Ernest Ford's youth, these same men represented the very antithesis of the lessons of courage, honesty, humility and brotherhood that they endeavored so hard to ingrain in their sons. When Ernest learned his father had refused a local chapter's efforts to recruit him, his explanation, and its inherent lesson were unequivocal, and were etched into Ernest Ford's heart and mind for the rest of his life: *'Anyone who claims to be doing God's work but hides their face under a hood is a coward.'*

Years later, Dad told me that moment convinced him that his father, "…was the bravest man I ever knew. With all my heart, I lived my life hoping to emulate him and the courage he showed me that day."

More than thirty years later, that hope and courage would be put to the test in Ernest Ford's own life.

. . . .

In the summer of 1965, America was on fire.

The fuses lit in the spring in Alabama burned like phosphorescent cables of primacord from Montgomery to Selma, to Birmingham and beyond. From sea to shining sea we watched on our Philcos and Zeniths from the comfort and safety of our dens, our kitchens and our bedrooms as Martin Luther King led great multitudes of the faithful and the disenfranchised on marches protesting the lack of the most basic of civil rights; marches led in the face of hatred and state troopers and police; and we watched as the firehoses and the tear gas and the dogs and the billy clubs were turned on them all; men, women, and children alike.

Like living etchings, black and white news footage and stark images of Bloody Sunday and the Pettus Bridge and Selma and Montgomery were burned into the nation's collective retina. Battle lines were drawn in cities and towns and diners and living rooms across the country. Racial equality and injustice drove the national discourse. Families were riven apart, and it seemed the fate of the nation's very soul hung in the balance. Great caravans of organizers, voting rights lawyers, medics, and the enlightened traveled from all points in the country to Alabama to join the swelling ranks of national figures, celebrities and average white Americans, marching arm-in-arm with black brothers and sisters across those lines the very men in hoods and sheets had worked so hard for so long to draw.

And we watched it all unfold on the nightly news.

Which is what Clarence and Maude Ford—like thousands of others—were doing three months later in the living room of their home in Bristol when a local news affiliate broadcast a story covering a Klan cross-burning in Kingsport, a little more than twenty miles away.

Grainy, backlit with a cordon of headlights and torches, a great white cross, swathed in kerosene-soaked burlap stood rooted in the ground, anchored by guywires strung taut and surrounded by a phalanx of hooded ranks and families of locals.

It was a scene they were not unfamiliar with; with the increased national attention on the movement for civil rights, sanctioned and county-permitted cross-burnings were ramped up coast-to-coast, as the Klan's best answer to that rising tide, and their own form of 'protest'. Like perverted shadows of Bible camp meetings, they took on the guise of Christian gatherings, passing tithing plates, taking collections, having dinner on the ground, and, as the lighting began, singing the hymns of the churches of their people.

They'd seen it all before.

But this burning and this broadcast would be different, and would have an indelible impact on not only Clarence and Maude, but on thousands of others, and, more than twenty-three hundred miles away, on Ernest Ford. A burning that would leave a scar that would never fully heal, and set the stage for a quiet battle that would give him that opportunity to know whether he'd learned the lesson of courage his father had taught him thirty-seven years earlier.

On the screen of the Magnavox console, Clarence and Maude watched as a pair of men mounted loudspeakers atop a pair of trucks, and a trio of robed and hooded Klansmen marched toward the cross, each bearing a long, pitched torch, the flames writhing high above them. Around them, virtually all movement and activity ceased as the believers turned almost as one towards the flame-illuminated triad. As they held their torches aloft, an elder spoke through the loudspeakers, urging the faithful to hold high the hymnal page they'd been given, and join together in the singing of the hymn, *'The Old Rugged Cross'*. From the loudspeakers, the unmistakable sound of a needle settling into the grooves of a disc could be heard from a portable record player, then, an instrumental refrain that felt familiar, and then, a voice singing the first lines of the first verse; lines known by everyone who'd ever sung the song, in church or elsewhere, lines sung now by a voice known by millions.

The voice of their son—my father—Ernest Ford.

. . . .

I rarely saw my father truly angry. Save for once, I never saw or heard him lose his temper, or raise his voice in rage or indignation. But this event taxed even his normally quiet, if smoldering resolve, and pushed him to a point where he knew he had a choice to make. I accepted then, as I do now, that he'd never have joined Tony Bennett, or Harry Belafonte on the Freedom Marches, that it was unlikely he'd ever link arms in solidarity with Dr. King or James Lewis or add his name to the lineup of any concerts for civil rights. He wasn't cut from that cloth. But to have done nothing would've invited acquiescence, and the linking of his name to the same body of hate that his father had quietly stood against.

Instead, he chose another path of recourse, one he was counseled to take on the advice of his attorneys, his accountants, and his record label; one that would hit the Imperial Knights of the Ku Klux Klan where they were most vulnerable.

Their bank accounts.

What the Klan had unknowingly done was violated one of the oldest laws on the books: misappropriating one's likeness, voice, or name for profit, without permission. They would cease and desist immediately with an issued apology and statement denying Ernest

Ford's affiliation on any level, or see their funding coffers disappear in a court battle they could never win; the evidence of their action literally seen by thousands.

By August, the national press had picked up the story, by September, the Klan had issued an apology, and by year's end, the matter was no longer news.

I don't know if my father was what you'd call a brave man, but I know that to have done nothing would have robbed him of any hope of knowing whether he measured up to the quiet strength, conviction and courage his father showed him those many years before. I believe that in his own way, he met that test, and would've made his father proud.

As I am today.

Know Thine Enemy, Know Thyself

Spring 2014

JBuck Ford

Know Thine Enemy, Know Thyself

Sometime in the long hours before dawn, I hit the ON button on the remote and groped for my glasses as the flat screen faded on, peeling back the darkness in the den, flickering to life in the middle of act two of *Jaws*; Brodie, Hooper and Quint in the *Orca's* cabin, half in the bag over a bottle of rum. The hull creaking under them as the boat pitches and yaws in the night, Quint and Hooper swapping stories about their adventures on the high seas, laughing off the danger they've both faced, and the wounds to prove it.

It is a telling moment of acceptance between the two characters.

But the moment's timbre and temper drop along with the laughter as Quint slowly, quietly, tells Hooper and Brodie of having been a survivor of the torpedo attack on *The Indianapolis* in 1944. Of desperately trying to hold a circle of men together in the open sea while they waited for rescue, and the horror of watching nearly all ripped to pieces one at a time, and taken to the depths by the sharks.

In the near-quiet of the cabin, the terrible truth of Quint's story is viscerally powerful. But as I watched, my eyes shifted to Hooper, sitting behind him, listening. Brilliantly, silently played by Richard Dreyfus, the power of Quint's words are virtually written across Hooper's face. Together, Hooper, Brodie, and we are being told of a great and terrible secret in a man's life; one we learn still carries a price. It is the first time we see the truth of the man behind his armor, and we know that he, and indeed, everything, is not what it seems.

In the half-light of the den, lying half awake, I recalled something Dreyfus said some years after the film, about his preparation for that scene. *You see Quint's whole life in his telling of that one story*, I remembered him saying. He thought about a verse Plato had written, Dreyfus said— that, *'Everyone you meet is fighting a battle you know nothing about'*.

It was all he focused on, he said. We can't always pick all our battles or our enemies, he said. Powerful words to live by, he said.

For years now, they've been words that have literally kept me alive. More than once. From an enemy no less of a killer, in a battle I have kept secret from all but a very few. A battle waged in darkness and fought in shadow, with an enemy you cannot see.

. . . .

I have been in the grip of a powerful and unforgiving depression for more than six years as I write this. Longer, I suspect, though I didn't know what name to put to it when I first felt its shadow fall about me. An insidious thing, depression; relentless and wholly evil, it is an enemy you cannot eliminate, only pray to manage, one struggle at a time. It pulls the very will to breathe out of you, and convinces you of the pointlessness of doing so, even if the will was there. I was in its grasp before I was conscious of it, and have only a vague recollection of awakening one day, one hour, empty of all happiness, vacant of all hope, contemplating the wisdom or the folly, the blessing or the sin, of taking my own life. A decision I was spared; the price the thing exacted from me took care of that.

For nearly twenty years, mine had been a life largely marked by death. In February of 1989, after three failed suicide attempts, my mother wrote a bitter goodbye note to Dad, washed three scrip bottles of trancs down with a water glass full of vodka, and died two days after. Two years later, after forty years of alcoholism, six years of liver failure and two years of dementia, Dad was gone.

In January of '94, his sixty-six year old heart weakened beyond repair from six attacks in less than twenty years, we buried Murph's father.

Five years and eight months later, our oldest son, Patrick, was killed when his Crown Vic hit the Eavins Creek bridge abutment twenty feet from the DeKalb County line, head on. He was six months shy of twenty-one.

In the spring of 2008, Murph's younger brother, Steve, piped in a fingernail's worth of blow and threw the cardiac switch, killing him at 44.

Nine months later, I lost my only brother, Brion, his chest cavity and spinal cord suffocated in the clutch of eight cancerous tumors, incubated over a lifetime of bourbon, smokes and pharmaceuticals, coiled inside him like a nest of snakes, revealed and diagnosed only a few months before he died. He was fifty-six. At some point on one side or the other of burying him, my thirty-year long marriage went into a coma and onto life-support. It hasn't spoken an intelligible sentence since. On nights I was able to actually fall asleep, I'd drift off certain that it, too, would be dead and gone when and if I awakened in the morning.

By the time I wrapped the last legs of the tour for my first book, I'd become anathema to the people I cared most deeply for, the people who were and are my very breath, my life itself.... my family.

I'd hidden this thing from all those I loved, not wishing to shake whatever faith they might still have had in me as a father and husband, friend and teacher. For much of my life, I sought to be the rock that others could lean on, to be emotionally strong when faith and hope slipped from my family's grasp. To be the man, the harbor, the stone, the strength. The refuge. The authority. The father. The one who doesn't flinch, the one who is never afraid. The one who will carry them through corridors of darkness until the light finally appears.

But I had lost my footing and my way, and my will. I was consumed by darkness and grief. I saw no light, and I felt no love any longer. My strength was gone. I cursed my weakness, and my self-ishness, ashamed in knowing that I needed help when my family and so many others fighting so many battles so many times worse, needed mine.

This was not happening to me. This was not *going* to happen to me. In the fall of '09 when a doctor pulled a chair alongside mine, opened a manila folder and said, "You're suffering from severe, clinical depression...", I looked around the room convinced she was talking to and about someone else. Who the hell is she talking about? *What* the hell is she talking about? I am a man... strong and resilient. Depression is.... weaker than me. I am a sixth degree black belt, for God's sake. Forged in the fire of Bushido, impervious to infective adversaries like depression. Yudansha are the shoulders for others to cry on, for others to stand on.

But this enemy cares nothing for the color of obis, or of the skin, or the strength of will or of spirit one has. It lies in wait in the shadows of grief and sorrow; patient, reptilian. Silent. It wraps you immobile in coils of bitterness and anger, slowly constricting your life away. It doesn't care who you are, where you're from, what you do, or what life you lead.

It plays no favorites. It brooks no quarter.

....

Over the past four years, I've been told that controlling this foe would require therapy. Long sessions of therapy. And drugs. Heavy drugs. Antidepressant pharmaceuticals with names I have to read twice and litanies of side-effects that bring into question the sanity of anyone willing to take them. 'It may be the only way to keep the depression at bay....at a distance," I was told. "To recover. To regain your Self."

I eschewed both, choosing instead to pull this enemy even closer. To listen for its approach. To know its shape, and recognize its shadow. If it could not be vanquished, it could be understood. If I could learn what this enemy was, I could learn to defeat it. I would look into its eyes, and I would know its name.

Knowledge is power.

But when I looked into those depths, I did not see the monster I expected. I did not see the shifting, coiling thing I'd felt around me for so long. What I saw were my own eyes. And I knew. I knew that the darkness that had surrounded me for these long years was of my own making.

At the risk of going all literary here, I had met the enemy, and it was me.

I had failed to move past the griefs in my life, believing that if I did, I would be forsaking those I'd lost, burying the memories of their beautiful lives with them; something I could not bring my-self to do. Instead, I wrapped their deaths around me; cloaks of pain and loss that kept me in shadow, blind to the anguish I was causing in those closest to me, and to the battles they were fighting. I knew that if I did not walk out of the darkness I'd made, I would lose them as well, and never know, or be able to defend them in the battles that they were fighting.

. . . .

Today, the shadow still lingers in the corners of my thoughts. Its strength has not dimmed or lessened, and I do not prevail in every battle I fight with it. But in the brightness of life, in the truth of knowing that everyone we meet is fighting a battle we know nothing about, our own shadows seem less powerful, and cannot last in the light of day.

The Epigraph, the Prayer,
and the Hawk

Fall, 2021

The Epigraph, the Prayer,
and the Hawk

February, 1976

SILENT, COCOONED, THE CITY LAY UNDER a four inch quilt of fresh snow, with another three looked for before morning. Flakes the size of half-dollars filled the grey of the night, floating lazily downward as light as feathers, their numbers so vast I could hear the whispers of their touch as they lit atop the white drifts already on the ground.

Gloved and capped against the cold, I stood sentry on our apartment's second-floor balcony, peering through the rippling curtain of falling snow, watching nervously for the cab I'd called earlier— the result of our once-reliable, Forest Green 76 Pinto Hatchback's sudden death only two days before. Below me, it sat buried among the other vehicles in the complex parking lot, each an all-but-indistinguishable white mound, forming a long, snow-covered hedgerow of metal and glass and rubber, the phalanx of sideview mirrors like miniature wings on a mothballed fleet, the roofs lit across their tops now from the approaching lights of the taxi.

In the living room, less than an hour away from her water breaking, Murph sat wedged in the cane rocker we'd salvaged from a yard sale, an overnight bag and a purse beside her, and she, encased in a knee-length down parka, as if wearing a sleeping bag, albeit one barely big enough to make it around her belly. I grasp her wrists and plant my feet and slowly pull her out of the rocker. We file down the condo stairwell to the landing and cut a trail through the drifts outside the portico to the open rear door of the cab. Armed with years of doctoring livestock on the ranch under my belt, I ease Murph into the back seat of the big National, lay her down, pillow her up and buckle her in, stow the overnight bag on the floorboard, open the front passenger door and climb in shotgun next to the cabbie. He cranes his neck back towards Murph, and throws it reverse. The big rear 750x16's just spin on the snowpack, the cab rocking against the drifts, the whine of the tires coming up through the chassis floor. "This your first?" he hollers.

. . . .

Nineteen years later, I was standing in front of the footlocker we'd stored his clothes in the week before. Upon two short flat-topped stools it lay; a long and faded black backboard box with tarnished brass-plated fixtures and knobbed brass corner guards. Stitched leather grips riveted to the side plates at each end. The lid a palette of rock band decals and alt logos.

I laced the fingers of my hands together in a futile attempt to keep them from trembling. Breathed deeply and opened them. Balled them into fists then opened them again. Moved them to the round releases at each end of the trunk, and with my thumbs, slid them across the plates, snapping open both latches. The *sla-tack* of the hasps releasing and striking the latch-plate above both of them sounded with a dull echo in the room, like hammers coming down on empty revolvers. Like a pair of switches thrown, stopping the passage of time and the flow of blood in my veins. Slowing the very molecules in the air.

Unmoving, unwilling, I stood rooted in fear, the tips of my fingers resting on the corners of the trunk's lid until I felt the breath return to my body. Then slowly (the thing impossibly heavy), I raised the lid.

The scent of his body, of his breath, exhaled from the locker as if I'd opened an ancient sepulcher, washing over me, blinding my eyes and taking my very breath away. Like a penitent, I dropped to my knees and gripped the edge of the crate, struggling to see for the tears streaming from my eyes, and struggling to stop them. Like springs they ran, unabated, coursing down my face and my neck and falling to the floor.

I know now that it was then, that it was in that instant, that blink in time, that I was broken.

....

I have been attempting off and on for more than five years, now, to write these lines. I've filled legal pads with passages and paragraphs, notes and recollections, thoughts and ideas, but all feel incomplete.

I've spent hours upon hours—days—researching and reading books and essays about grief and loss, but all seem distant and separate from my own. I've devoured how-to manuals on how to express that grief and write about it. I've immersed myself in the prose of Joan Didion. I've sought therapy, with the hope that I might break through and find the way in, but inevitably, after only so much laboring, I've simply stopped. The pain and uncertainty of what I'm trying to do overwhelm me. Where to begin, how to begin. I move between worlds. Between the living and the dead. I wash myself in waters of regret and sorrow. I seek answers to questions I fear to ask. I try to make sense of the chaos that pain and guilt have made of my life. I struggle with the thought that asking someone to read about the passing of our son and the anguish we've known is the penultimate act of selfishness and vanity.

. . .

I have no great secret to reveal in this writing, no salve that might soothe anyone's dolor or heartache. I do not put pen to this paper because I have lessons to share or help to offer. No *How I Learned to Cope with the Loss of a Child* advice. It has been twenty-two years now and the pain of his death is as deep and ragged and open as it has been since the night I looked upon his body.

No—I put this pen to paper for different reasons; both born, at least partly, out of fear. Fear that as I grow older, I am slowly forgetting. Forgetting the feel of his face, the part of his hair. The glide of his gait and the easy roll of his laughter. Fear that the long list of the sins of my life will be not be measured and exacted in purgatorial recompense after my death, but from my living memory of my firstborn. Of the arc of brilliance that was his life. Of his strength, his weaknesses, of the lessons I learned from him too late.

And so, now, here in this long autumn of my own life, I put this pen to paper and I reach back to remember. I rifle through the banker's boxes, pore through file folders and envelopes and find the few photographs I kept. I arrange them by his age, by where he is, who he's with; by the size of the picture. But the images all begin to flow into each other. I'm looking into a time machine, losing my focus and my tether to the present. I scan them, shoot them with my iPhone and save them in folders on my hard drive. I create panels and organize them, hoping that by converting them, and sorting them, perhaps I'll see them clearer somehow. That I'll see *him* clearer. I place the photographs on the table and arrange them just so; each a window, and I look through them and I plumb the depths of my heart and my memory and hope to remember.

I call up the ghosts and pray I remember.

. . . .

We'd been home from the service for less than an hour, the week all but a blur, our strength all but gone. Surrounded by the family and our closest friends, we sat under a slow-moving ceiling fan on the back porch and ate and talked and remembered and wept, our hearts broken beyond repair.

As the daylight faded, and the last shadows lay across the ground, my eyes fixed on a panel of the shadowbox fence surrounding the yard. A fence we'd built just five years earlier. A fence I knew every inch of. But the 4x4 post I was looking at was one I couldn't have set in the ground because it was two feet taller than every other post on the line.

I began to stand, intending to walk the eighty feet to the fence, but as I did, the top of the post seemed to… move. To shift, as if turning on a spindle. Slowly, I sat back down, the conversation fading to silence around me, and rested my hand on Murph's, nodding towards the fence.

"Look," I said.

And as the word left my mouth, the figure shifted again, now visible in a last light of the day, a great red-tailed hawk it was, its colors and markings brilliant in the alpenglow, its eyes regarding us almost as if it knew us.

Transfixed, none of us dared move, locked in a moment that seemed to stretch out interminably. Then, as if in slow motion, its wings unfolded, lifting it off aloft where it seemed to hover in mid-air, and then, as if homing on us, it wings pumped and the great bird flew directly towards us, breaking off only at the last second before disappearing into the darkening sky above. But as it did, a single feather broke from an outstretched wing and fell—gyring in the breeze and landing at the base of the fence upon the green lawn.

. . . .

I have carried this feather with me for twenty-two years, now, its shape and hue undiminished by time. If the Native American legend is true, we were given a message that day; one that still echoes in my memory these long years later. A message that bids me bide my time, that one day I will remember, and we will all be soaring....

I miss you, son.

The Afterword, the Acknowledgements
and the Thanks

THE ARC OF MY LIFE has been one of perpetual change, whether I was ready for that change or not. Over the years, plot points I carefully devised, and mistakenly believed I could drop seamlessly in the storyline, as well as those I had no hand in creating, spun the narrative time and again, requiring the abandonment of any and all best-laid plans and rough drafts.

But the one constant, the one saving grace, were those souls who were there to help navigate the new directions; the guides who put the maps in my hand and pointed the way, the writers whose work and words lit the darkened corners, the colleagues and clients who gave me the opportunities, who gave me a shot.... who gave me their faith and trust. Every move forward I've been lucky enough to make—every new draft of the manuscript— has been with the help of those souls in whose debt I remain; a cast of supporting characters too numerous to list, who have changed the arc of my life in ways too countless to mention.

I am a man most richly blessed.

JBuck Ford ~ Nashville. January 1, 2025

About the Author

JBuck Ford is a writer, producer and content creator based in Nashville, Tennessee and Los Angeles, California. His first book, *'River of No Return ~ Tennessee Ernie Ford and the Woman He Loved'* was called "Masterfully rendered…compulsively readable and… fascinating." by Publishers Weekly in their starred review.

'Ghost in This House ~ essays from a privileged life' is his second book.

Be sociable

jbuckford.com

facebook.com/JBuckFord

instagram.com/jbuckford/

youtube.com/@jbuckfordtv

Also by JBuck Ford

RIVER of NO RETURN - **Tennessee Ernie Ford and the Woman He Loved /** (Turner Books)

"[A] masterfully rendered biography. Compulsively readable and... fascinating." *Publishers Weekly (Starred Review)*

"Other biographies cannot emit the raw emotion and intimate details…in this well-written and compelling memoir." *Library Journal'*

"Heartwarming and heart-wrenching…I couldn't put it down." *Tab Hunter*

"I was touched by the truth, love, pain and honesty of this book." *Maureen O'Hara*

"A top pick..." *Midwest Book Review*

Available on Amazon and at all bookstores

What we do is what we are.